NEW ORLEANS DINING:
A Guide for the Hungry Visitor
Craving an Authentic Experience

2012 Edition

Written Without Reservations by
Steven Wells Hicks

Fiction by Steven Wells Hicks

The Gleaner
The Fall of Adam
Horizontal Adjustment

This book's ISBN-13 is 978-1468065671 and ISBN-10 is 146806567X.

To query about permissions for advertising and / or other text usage,
please contact the author at mail@stevenwellshicks.com

For The Sensible One

Sacred cows make the best hamburger.

-- *Mark Twain (attributed)*

WELCOME TO THE SECOND edition of *New Orleans Dining*.

This year's edition contains twelve new entries, replacing seven entries from the original 2011 edition. That's not to say the new places are necessarily better than those deleted; they're just different.

In a lot of ways, books like this can be a lot like sex.

The process of experiencing, thinking and writing about restaurants is almost as personal and certainly as subjective as lovemaking.

Everyone has their own ideas about what makes it great, and those ideas are seldom the same. No one knows if they're really good at it, but everyone likes to think (or at least hope) they are. With experience, people begin to think they're really getting the hang of it. And, oh yes, some people have far kinkier tastes than others.

This book is written unapologetically for visitors.

One of the first things anyone in the tourism industry learns is that most visitors to a new place, no matter why they're travelling, want to have an authentic experience. That generally translates into seeing, doing and tasting things that are indigenous or unique to the destination.

That is particularly true when it comes to dining. Sure, if you gather enough people together, there will be one or two poor souls who want to visit the golden arches or have food be prepared exactly the way they like it at home. Why these people travel at all bewilders me.

Others will want to visit the latest chi-chi bistro that's all the buzz, the type of place where the latest madman to don a chef's tunic is waxing rhapsodic about lizard lips flashed in liquid nitrogen.

All of that is well and good, but such disparate alternatives certainly fail to capture the essence of New Orleans, which is a city that is old, gracious and steeped in homegrown culinary traditions. For forty years, friends around the country have asked me, as a visiting outsider myself, to recommend places offering those types of experiences. And that's exactly what this guidebook is – a personal journal of forty years of culinary escapades in one of America's legendary dining cities armed with little more than a fork, a taste for indigenous foods and a thirst for homegrown authenticity.

About 97% of the city's restaurants aren't here.

New Orleans based food writer Tom Fitzmorris identifies more than 1200 places that meet "real restaurant" standards on his excellent blog (www.nolamenu.com). The ZAGAT Guide published in 2009 has 388 listings. This book contains 32 entries, and here's why:

1. Most people, and I'm guessing you're one of them, don't want to slog through that many listings when they're

trying to figure out a place to go for lunch or dinner.

2. In distilling forty years of mostly delectable "research" into a book designed to help you plan a single visit, I've tried to limit the selections to restaurants that are generally reflective of the city and its historical cuisines. There are some entries that people might consider exceptions – an over-the-top greasy spoon and a cozy wine bar on the West Bank among them – but I've tried to mainly stick with places that will give you some ideas about the city's cuisines and culinary heritage.

3. The shorter number of restaurants affords me the luxury of writing at greater length about each of them, allowing me to talk about what makes them unique: in some cases their history, in others the backgrounds of New Orleans classics that were created in their kitchens, or perhaps the overall "vibe" that so typifies the joyous spirit of the city.

The restaurants are neither ranked nor rated.

While I've been called handy in a kitchen, I don't pretend to be a food critic. My tastes are generally American Mainstream leaning toward the adventurous. Since we all carry prejudices and pre-conceived notions about what we eat, let me confess to a few of mine that have shaped my personal opinions over the decades. I think the culinary contributions of the French classicists are frequently overrated while the genius coming out of Italian and Spanish kitchens are all too often overlooked. I am far more impressed by simple foods exquisitely prepared than I am by exotic ingredients with hefty price tags.

Even more importantly, I believe it's both unfair and fool-ish to use the same scale to evaluate a white tablecloth tem-ple of cuisine, a 93 year-old neighborhood oyster bar, a fried chicken joint in a dicey section of the city and an undiscov-ered adjunct to a school lunchroom in a blue-collar part of town.

Finally, there are a few places for which I can work up nothing more but contempt, and words do such a better job of expressing unvarnished disdain than any numeric rank-ing ever could.

Why No Prices Are Included

If you're reading this in Des Moines, your points of refer-ence on restaurant prices will be considerably different from those of someone reading this in midtown Manhattan.

Prices on separate items within the same menu can vary wildly. Is a restaurant serving a seven buck po'bot sandwich and a sixty buck Porterhouse steak "moderate" or "family-priced" or "pricey?" You'll find places like that in New Or-leans, and so far the best answer I've been able to come up with on the price question is "Yes."
Generalizations about "average meals" are fuzzy math at best.

So, with the exception of breakfast at Brennan's for which I point out and take issue with specific prices, here is what I'll tell you about the costs of dining in New Orleans:

1. Because the industry is so competitive in New Orleans, prices are comparatively low for a major American city.

2. For the same item, chances are you'll pay more in New

York and less in Green Bay.

3. The more famous a restaurant's chef is, the more you're likely to pay.

4. More upscale restaurants tend to have à la carte menus, but many offset the need for a calculator with price fixe offerings as well.

5. As a rule of thumb, places outside the French Quarter and the Central Business District generally charge less than their brethren in the high-priced real estate. There are exceptions to this, of course, and some are noticeable. Within these pages you'll find profiles of Clover Grill, an openly gay greasy spoon in the heart of the French Quarter that pounds out good 24/7 chow at giveaway prices, and Mosca's, which is one of the city's pricier Creole-Italian restaurants even though it's a swamp-side roadhouse several miles from the middle of nowhere.

6. Taxes are relatively high on hospitality products and services in New Orleans, and until you get used to them, you may be in for a little jolt when the waitperson hands you your tab.

Like anywhere else, sticker shock is possible. In order to avoid it, I normally check a restaurant's website menu for prices. If they don't print the prices, I figure they know they're too high, so I'll usually avoid the restaurant.

Stuff to Pacify the Lawyers

This is ultimately a book of opinions, my own, based upon past and recent visits to the named restaurants and attendant observations. Supporting facts were gathered from websites, articles, cookbooks and other items listed in the Appendix section in the back of this book. If any article contains hard factual errors, historical of otherwise, I take full responsibility and offer my most sincere apology. If there's anything else I screwed up, I'm sorry about that, too. Letters of correction or complaint should be e-mailed to me at mail@stevenwellshicks.com. If you want to write a letter saying nice things about me, that's okay, too. I'll pass them on to my mom.

Enough said. Let's eat.

The ZERO POINT
How the guide is arranged.

If there is a center of the visitors and convention zone of the city, it would be at the intersection of Canal Street where Royal Street changes into St. Charles Avenue, which will be referred to in this guide as The Zero Point.

At that intersection, which separates the French Quarter and the Central Business District, it's possible for visitors to catch both the historic St. Charles and Canal Street streetcars, one of the last such systems still operating in the United States.

In the listings at the end of every restaurant piece, you'll find the mileage from The Zero Point to the restaurant.

Each of the five sections is arranged by distance from The Zero Point, nearest to farthest. Distances were calculated by Google maps. New Orleans can prove to be a confusing city for newcomers to walk or drive. If you have a smart phone, you might consider using your GPS or similar program.

Finally, while most of the restaurants in this guidebook are in "safer" parts of what can be a dangerous city, getting to them often requires going though sections of town that can get dicey. A good rule of thumb is, "If you don't know, don't walk. Take a cab."

The 2012 Bill of Fare

TEN THAT SET THE STANDARD
Galatoire's

K-Paul's

Bayona

Herbsaint

Mandina's

Parkway Bakery & Tavern

Casamento's

Brigtsen's

Mosca's

* La Provence

LOCAL FLAVOR
Central Grocery

Pascal's Manale

* R&O's

Drago's

* Brocato's Eat Dat

* Charlie's Seafood

SIZE MATTERS
Clover Grill

* Irene's Cuisine

* Vine& Dine

Willie Mae's

Lola's

LOWER YOUR EXPECTATIONS
Brennan's
* Café du Monde
* Palm Court Jazz Café
Commander's Palace
* The Camellia Grill

WALKING DISTANCE FAVORITES
Dickie Brennan's Steakhouse
* August
* Arnaud's
Napoleon House
* Croissant d'Or
The Dry Dock Cafe & Bar

(* denotes new for this edition)

Deleted from 2011 Edition:
Café Reconcile • Charlie's Steak House • Lola's
Middendorf's • Surrey's Juice Bar
The Ruby Slipper • Venezia

I.
THE TEN THAT
SET THE STANDARD

I'M NOT SURE anyone can confidently name the ten "best" restaurants in New Orleans. Many have tried, of course, and whether they have succeeded or failed is every bit as subjective on the part of the reader as it is on the writers who make up the lists.

The pure breadth of cultural influences and ingredients shaping the wide-ranging varieties of native New Orleans cooking make assembling a "ten best" list a fool's errand.

That said, the ten restaurants that follow were selected as premier examples of several indigenous types of New Orleans cuisine. Some may, and surely will, argue that one of the other "grand dame" temples of French Creole cuisine is superior to Galatoire's, that there's no sine qua non that separates Casamento's from any number of other oyster bars, or brand of voodoo that makes a shrimp "po'bo"y at Parkway Bakery and Tavern worth a special trip when there's another sandwich shop around the corner.

Others could argue that several of the restaurants in the "Local Color" section of this guidebook should be included in this list rather than that.

All are legitimate arguments or sincere differences of opinion, both of which amount to a national sport in this city where the locals are as passionate about food and restaurants as Italians can be about opera or Brazilians are about soccer.

Where most people can agree is that the ten restaurants herein offer a combination of food, atmosphere and vibe that will steer the one-time or occasional visitor away from recognized tourist traps and instead point the city's guests toward places that live up to the city's remarkable dining reputation.

Galatoire's

All said, it is a room more accommodating to easy conversation than stiff formality, a place conducive to deciding the world will be better served with one more bottle of champagne than three more hours of work.

SOMETIMES EVENTS OCCUR close enough to each other that they lead people to suspect there must be some sort of cause-and-effect relationship between them.

Lately, I've found myself pondering the possible linkage of two seemingly incongruent facts. The first is the 1905 opening of Jean Galatoire's bistro in the building that had already housed Victor's restaurant for 75 years. The second occurred two years later, when an enterprising tailor around the corner from the bistro cut and stitched together the first two-piece seersucker suit.

While common sense may dictate that the seersucker suit was designed to offer gentleman a fashionable respite from the subtropical heat and brutal humidity of a New Orleans summer, I might consider a good-natured wager that the fellow who bought that original blue and white seersucker suit made a beeline from the tailor's shop to his standing Friday lunch at Galatoire's – and that five generations later, his great-great-great grandson is likely doing the same.

To declare Galatoire's the finest place for both a meal and

the opportunity to experience the graciousness of New Orleans is no stretch. If anything, it's predictable, perhaps even inevitable, but the reason for the restaurant's continuing acclaim is at once unusual, ephemeral and one of the most cherished attributes of the city herself.

The success of most restaurants is traditionally based upon the food they serve, yet any number of New Orleans eateries can lay claim to more innovative recipes and presentations than those that have been coming out of the Galatoire's kitchen for years. While some establishments base their success on the glittering reputations of up-and-coming superstar chefs, more than a century of chefs and line cooks have toiled in relative obscurity, if not outright anonymity, at Galatoire's.

Moreover, few local residents would quibble with the contention that numerous dining rooms exist in the city where the décor is more romantic or refined and the service is less daunting.

So what is the element, the sine qua non, that lifts Galatoire's to its lofty status as arguably the city's signature restaurant?

In a word, continuity.

On those most rare occasions when Galatoire's begrudgingly allows change to occur at all, the slightest alteration is undertaken with great trepidation by a management well conditioned to the fact that the most miniscule modification will be met with both choruses of harrumphs and howls of outrage from hidebound regulars who regard any break with tradition as the hand basket in which the world is being carted off to Hell.

As a result, the front doors at Galatoire's have become and remain a final barricade against a world that has become faster, harsher and increasingly ill mannered; a last bastion of both gentility and the camaraderie of neighborly table hopping between people who renew their friendships on a weekly basis.

Step out the doors, outside this coddling cocoon where champagne flutes clink and patrician waiters gently nudge patrons toward the day's freshest offerings, and you're sucked into the maelstrom of Bourbon Street with its jaded bump-and-grind of topless clubs, condom shops, clip joints, t-shirt emporia, fluorescent drinks, hot dog stands and teeming flocks of slack-jawed yokels taking it all in.

In 1911, when Jean Galatoire paid $25,000 for the building that houses his restaurant, it was shoehorned between a laundry and a genteel dress shop. The Storyville District, where jazz was born and sporting girls plied their trade in everything from Gilded Age parlors to clapboard cribs, was blocks away across Basin Street. Bourbon Street was still a setting where upright citizens needn't turn red-faced should they bump into their priests or preachers.

For over a century, Galatoire's has emphatically refused to move, or change very much of anything for that matter, and now finds itself a metaphoric tea rose atop a dung pile, a prince among frogs, an Andrew Wyeth egg tempera masterwork in a posterized Andy Warhol world.

From all appearances, Galatoire's hasn't even noticed the transition. Indeed, the restaurant quietly goes about its business, does things in its own long-established ways and, on its 100th anniversary in 2005, was cited as the Outstanding

Restaurant in the nation in the prestigious James Beard Foundation awards.

Consider the world as it was in 1905, when the restaurant's new owner was cutting the ropes used to display smoked hams and game in the storefront windows of Victor Bero's 75 year-old bistro, and nailing up the sign that would evermore designate the building at 209 Bourbon Street as Galatoire's.

Theodore Roosevelt was living in the building he renamed "The White House." Ragtime was all the musical rage. In Pittsburgh, the death knell sounded for the nickelodeon when the first modern movie theatre opened to packed houses spellbound by the flickering fourteen-minute Western, The Great Train Robbery. It was the year Albert Einstein reinvented physics with the simple formula $e=mc2$, Ernest Hemingway was a schoolboy and a woman could still get two cents back after buying a quart of milk for a dime.

The earth has logged more than 38,000 rotations since Galatoire's opened is doors. America has fought six wars and been led by eighteen presidents. Yet rock steady in the swirling winds of history, Galatoire's has managed to change hardly at all.

Yes, there have been adjustments, small concessions to unstoppable progress and changing tastes. Air conditioning ultimately replaced fans blowing across ice blocks. Neckties for gentlemen became no longer required, but any man without a jacket after five or anytime Sunday can expect to be offered a coat from the foyer rack, or graciously escorted back through the front doors and once again to the sidewalk of Bourbon Street. After ninety years as a cash-only establishment, the restaurant finally gave in several years ago and started to begrudgingly accept credit cards.

A 1999 renovation moved the front doors to a side foyer and eliminated the airlock that partially shielded Tennessee Williams' regular table from public view, thereby allowing the eccentric playwright to indulge in catty gossip or snipe at other diners entering or leaving the room.

After a suitable period of agonized hand-wringing and teeth gnashing, most changes are eventually accepted by Galatoire's regulars with a certain amount of aplomb, but not always. When a particularly popular waiter was fired after being sued for sexual harassment, enraged regulars wrote such incendiary letters to The Times-Picayune that a local theatrical troupe assembled them into an hour-long play. Management's decision to thoughtlessly install a mechanical ice shaver, thereby ending the time-honored practice of having employees chip ice by hand, caused customer rumblings about a narrowly avoided mutiny of Potemkin proportions.

Resistance to change is so fervently embraced by both the owners and regular customers of Galatoire's that their relationship has emerged as irrevocably symbiotic, and this celebration of all things status quo is even reflected in the restaurant's extensive menu, where it is far easier to find a traditional French-Creole offering dating back to 1905 than to find one that doesn't.

An item has to fall so far out of culinary favor to be removed from the wide-ranging menu that very few have ever been, giving it a quaint charm with the inclusion of items like sheepshead, a flat-toothed fish that looks far more appealing on a plate than the bony thing ever did in the sea.

New additions to the menu come equally slowly. Consider two items that have become New Orleans standards that are yet to appear on Galatoire's menu. It's been over a quarter century since Paul Prudhomme launched a national craze for Louisiana cooking with blackened redfish from K-Paul's on Chartres Street. Drago's signature charbroiled oysters made their first appearance at the Cvitanovitch family's Metairie restaurant in 1993 and have since been knocked off by dozens of local places. Yet neither dish is yet to grace the pages of the lengthy Galatoire's menu.

Most new items to appear on the menu have been created in the Galatoire's kitchen by either staff or members of the Galatoire family, some of whom continue to work with the restaurant despite the sale of its majority interest in 2010. Crabmeat Yvonne was named for the founder's granddaughter, who started working behind the cashier's desk when a regular worker called in sick in 1938 and eventually became the company's president, serving until her death in 2000. It is a simple dish, five sautéed ingredients that can be presented as either a main course or prepared as a garnish for a surprising number of entrées.

The Godchaux Salad was named after Leon Godchaux, who in the 1920s would walk to lunch at Galatoire's daily from his elegant, eponymous department store on nearby Canal Street. During the scorching summer heat, the merchant would request a salad made from his favorite ingredients – iceberg lettuce, boiled shrimp, lump crabmeat, anchovies, vine-ripened tomatoes and a Creole mustard vinaigrette. Today, ninety years later, the salad is still a main-stay on the menu.

One of the restaurant's signature appetizers, the Crab-meat Canapé Lorenzo, was named after the neighborhood pharmacist. Jumbo lump crabmeat is folded into a tradi-tional Béchamel sauce with scallions, parsley, butter, egg yolks and seasoned with butter and both white and cayenne pepper. The mixture is next coated with breadcrumbs and grated Parmesan, and then spread on a toast round. Finally, anchovy filets are criss-crossed on top and finished to an earthy brown in the broiler.

The vast majority of the cuisine served at Galatoire's has its roots in the fundamentals of French or Creole cooking, which the restaurant has merged over the years into the hy-brid they call, not surprisingly, French Creole. Because of New Orleans' location near the Gulf of Mexico, there is a natural emphasis on fish and shellfish, but that certainly doesn't preclude the same attention paid – and creativity ap-plied – to a panoply of meat, game, poultry and even egg dishes.

Like the restaurant itself, the food is time-tested and tra-ditional rather than highly imaginative. It has been repeat-edly prepared and adjusted to the point that the master recipes don't change because there's no longer any need.

Over the course of a century, foods originated by other restaurants have found their way onto the Galatoire's menu, most notably Oysters Rockefeller, crisp yet puffy soufflé po-tatoes and pompano en papillote, all created by Antoine's, the city's oldest extant restaurant dating back to 1840. When two restaurants have a combined 278 years of experience, it is expected that each will cultivate its own group of devotees, and when Antoine's regulars like to remind those from Galatoire's that a dish was invented at Antoine's, they can expect to hear the reply, "Yes, but it was perfected at Galatoire's."

While Galatoire's menu is both long and wide-ranging, an examination of the restaurant's elegant cookbook published in 2005 reveals that the recipes are simpler than one might expect, the cooking times quicker and the ingredient lists shorter. One of the core reasons for this, the restaurant freely admits, is the superiority of ingredients arriving daily from the legion of purveyors with whom Galatoire's has forged relationships now calculable in generations.

For the past dozen years, Galatoire's has been operating on both the first and second floors of their building on Bourbon Street, the second floor having been reopened as part of the 1999 renovation. The second floor had been a colorful element of the restaurant's early years. A cluster of several small rooms, referred to as the chambres privées, it had been used for private parties, quite often circumspect assignations for two. A private entrance and discreet staff kept downstairs clientele abuzz with conjecture regarding the identities and whispers about the activities taking place over their heads. The city's scandalmongers must have been heartbroken when the rooms closed during World War II. The upstairs rooms today are very public and the only part of the restaurant that will accept reservations. They are rarely filled to capacity, since the heart of Galatoire's is clearly to be found in the first floor dining room below.

At first glance, the downstairs room looks as if it might

have been plucked from a Parisian bistro circa 1900. Despite tuxedoed waiters and often impeccably dressed patrons, there is not what most people would describe as an air of elegance in the room.

The floors are tile, the chairs bent wood, the walls bedecked with curved brass coat hooks and large mirrors above panels of white wainscot. Above the mirrors is rich green wallpaper with gold fleur de lis hand stenciling. Twin bladed fans lazily revolve from the ceiling.

In the back of the room, next to the kitchen entrance, a crisply dressed manager surveys the scene from behind an antique cashier's station, above which is a tall pendulum clock that marks the passage of hours with its stately chime.

All said, it is a room more accommodating to easy conversation than stiff formality, a place conducive to deciding the world will be better served with one more bottle of champagne than three more hours at work. Despite the grand clock's chiming, there are few places better suited for paying no attention to time.

First time visitors to Galatoire's would do well to remember one simple rule, which will assure a pleasurable and memorable experience: Trust your waiter. Some are as much of an institution at the restaurant as turtle soup or Poached Trout Margurey. Although their numbers have been diminishing through retirement or passing away, it wasn't all that long ago when seven members of one extended Cajun family worked the floor at the same time.

A waiter's position at Galatoire's is not a job, but rather a lucrative career to those who ply it. When asked, your waiter will quietly inform you of what looks best in the kitchen that particular day or may subtly shake his or her head should you order an item that might be better on another day. For visitors to whom the language of a French Creole kitchen is unfamiliar, the waiter can become an indispensable guide, explaining a dish or technique in such an affable manner it's difficult to believe it's his ten thousandth time.

While some visitors and guidebooks have referred to the corps working the front of the house as "condescending" or even "dictatorial," I have found their behavior to be a fairly accurate reflection of their patron. A cold or arrogant customer will be politely treated, of course, but with a chilling reserve. On the other hand, a guest who is friendly and curious will soon be treated like the newest member of an extended, happy family.

Regular guests soon request "their" waiter and the line separating server and those being served first blurs, then evaporates. The Sensible One and I were fortunate enough to have one of the seven Cajun waiters, Louis LaFleur from Ville Plat, as "our" waiter for fifteen years. It didn't take long before, upon our entrance, Louis would arrive with a chilled bottle of Veuve Clicquot, a report on the supply and merit of the day's lump crabmeat, stories about his family and complaints about his aching feet. Until his passing, we referred to lunch at Galatoire's as "a visit with Louis."

While the restaurant's traditions rarely change, and then are merely tweaked, there is one tradition destined to stay in place for as long as the Galatoire name remains above the canopy. It is a tradition that embraces fundamental equality while exposing the inherent arrogance of people who regard it as something for everyone else.

That tradition is "the line."

While the upstairs room now accepts reservations, the policy in the more desired downstairs remains no reservations, no exceptions. There is a famous story of former United States Senator J. Bennett Johnston being brought into the restaurant from deep in the line to accept a phone call from then President Ronald Reagan and upon the call's completion returning to his place in line.

There is another story I've heard numerous times with various names over the years, a story that's most likely apocryphal, but one that illustrates the restaurant's ironclad adherence to its policy. Legend has it that French president Charles de Gaulle was in New Orleans and appeared at Galatoire's door with an entourage. When politely told how happy the establishment was to see him, but that he would need to take his place in line like everyone else, the former commander of the French army supposedly asked if the host knew who he was. "Oui, Monsieur President," the host is purported to have answered, "but do you know where you are?" The anecdote ends with de Gaulle storming away in a Gallic snit. Over the years, I've heard the names of the Duke of Windsor, William Randolph Hearst and others used in place of the French general, and I doubt the veracity of any of them, but people who know Galatoire's and its rules know just how believable such a scenario is.

In recent years, particularly in advance of the legendary Friday lunches, a regrettable practice has not only started, but flourished – the use of "placeholders" – people hired to spend Friday mornings standing in line so their employers can replace them five minutes before the doors open, thereby avoiding the need to endure a long wait like the rest of humanity.

The fact that Galatoire's allows such an elitist system to survive is, at least to me, as bewildering as it is disgraceful. To the restaurant's defense, however, for the two busiest Fridays every year, those before Christmas and Fat Tuesday (Mardi Gras), Galatoire's has initiated auctions for tables and seating with proceeds going to local charities.

Friday lunches at Galatoire's have become a much written about tradition in New Orleans. During the summer months, you will see any number of men wearing seersucker or bow ties despite the loosened dress code. A handful of women will wear large, elegant hats and air kisses will be blown from table to table as freely as doubloons are thrown at a Carnival parade. Martini glasses will clink, wine bottles will be uncorked in prodigious numbers, platters of food will cascade out of the kitchen and from time to time, a waiter will clink a knife against a water glass to announce birthdays and lead the entire room in singing. It is not uncommon for the revelry to last all afternoon and often through dinner. This has led to an unofficial motto, "Come for lunch, stay for dinner, go home in a wheelbarrow."

From my point of view, however, Friday lunches at Galatoire's are an event that a visitor would be wiser to skip. Over the years, I've been to a healthy number of them. The food has been up to the high standard, the drinks icy, the service both friendly and crisp, and everyone as pleasant as they can be. But Fridays at Galatoire's are ultimately the province of clockwork regulars and insiders, a Petrie dish for social inbreeding New Orleans style. While visitors are certainly welcome, they will soon discover that the party swirls around them rather than includes them. They won't be on the outside looking in; they'll be on the inside looking in, much like a stepchild at a particularly close family's reunion.

For visitors wishing to absorb the whole Galatoire's experience, two elements are necessary; the first thing is a mind open to the idea that newer isn't always better and, secondly, time itself.

If you let down your guard and open your heart, you will be transported back a century into the last unruffled days of America's gilded age, but such a journey requires the time to savor it. I believe the shortest lunch The Sensible One and I ever enjoyed at Galatoire's lasted slightly over two hours. The longest went from 11:30 in the morning until 5:45 that afternoon, entailed three bottles of Veuve, two Crabmeat Canapé Lorenzos, turtle soup, Oysters Rockefeller, lamb chops Bernaise and Café Brulot, producing a bill that, even though Galatoire's prices are very reasonable considering both the quality and the cachet, could have underwritten a small European country.

Perhaps that marathon lunch was profligate, but I always wanted to feel like J.P. Morgan, John D. Rockefeller or any other self-respecting captain of American industry, and now I have.

Were I ever told that I would be allowed only one more New Orleans meal in my lifetime, I'd put on my seersucker suit and take my place in the legendary line that goes down Bourbon Street and often wraps around the corner. If you only have the opportunity for one memorable meal in "the city that care forgot," I recommend you do the same.

You'll find classic food, impeccable service and a room in which time can stand still if you make a point of ignoring the chiming of the clock. Just don't go looking for change, because they're fresh out.

Galatoire's
French Creole
209 Bourbon Street
(between Iberville and Bienville Streets)
0.1 mile by foot from The Zero Point
The downstairs dining room is open
Tuesday through Saturday
at 11:30 am. and on Sunday at noon
The restaurant closes at 10 p.m. and
is dark on Monday
All major credit cards honored;
reservations may be made for upstairs
Telephone: (504) 525-2021
Website: www.galatoires.com

K-Paul's Louisiana Kitchen

*The dish was christened "blackened" redfish, and it catapulted
Paul Prudhomme into the national culinary spotlight,
a place that seemed as comfortable to the man from Opelousas
as a bayou is to a gator.*

WHEN A LONG LINE FORMS ourside a New Orleans restaurant,
it can often prove amusing to observe the reactions of some
city residents. Should they know someone in line, they cite
it as proof that New Orleans is one big street party where the
locals sure know their food. Should they not, the restaurant
is pilloried as a tourist place unworthy of local patronage.

For more than fifteen years, Paul Prudhomme saw plenty
of the latter at the front door of K-Paul's, his runaway success of a restaurant in the French Quarter. When opened in
1979, the restaurant had a miniscule capacity of 62 guests,
creating the need for "community seating," the polite eu-
phemism for guests from more than one party being required to share a table with others. The arrangement was
tolerated when K-Paul's was only open at lunch, but when
the restaurant expanded its operation to serve dinner, people started to balk at the notion of sharing a relatively pricey
dinner with total strangers.

People grumbled and griped about seating and other
rules instituted to keep things manageable for the small

restaurant, but they kept flocking to K-Paul's because a revolution was taking place in Prudhomme's tiny kitchen.

For generations, diners in New Orleans had been hardwired into Creole cuisine, the refined style of cooking cobbled together from the foods of many nations, but with its underpinnings being predominantly French. The other Louisiana niche cuisine was Cajun, a heartier country style of cooking from Bayou Country, commonly dismissed as rustic by city dwellers. In fact, when Prudhomme opened K-Paul's in 1979, there was only one authentic Cajun restaurant of any real renown in New Orleans, the Bon Ton Café with roots going back to the early 1900s.

Prudhomme, the caboose of thirteen children from a Cajun farming family in Opelousas, spent a great part of his childhood cooking with his mother to feed the rest of the family, which worked the fields. He opened and closed a pair of restaurants before he was thirty and worked in kitchens across America before landing a job, at age 35, as the executive chef at Commander's Palace, which had just been taken over by the Brennans, New Orleans' family of celebrated restaurateurs.

It was at Commander's where Prudhomme's star shot skyward. By integrating Cajun ingredients and techniques into the Creole cuisine upon which the restaurant had built its reputation, Prudhomme created the new fusion cuisine that came to be generally known as "Louisiana" or "South Louisiana" cooking. While at Commander's, Prudhomme revised classic New Orleans recipes for the Brennans, including barbecue shrimp, turtle soup and others, a number of which are still served today in the family's various restaurants.

If Prudhomme's star was rising at Commander's, it was at K-Paul's where it went stratospheric, and it was primarily due to a remarkably simple idea that blended nine everyday herbs and spices, some butter and a piece of local fish in a black iron skillet so hot it literally smoked. The dish was christened "blackened" redfish, and it catapulted Paul Prudhomme into the national culinary spotlight, a place that seemed as comfortable to the man from Opelousas as a bayou is to a gator.

Prudhomme was a natural for television. A chef of tremendous girth at the time, he was a colorful man from a colorful place, gregarious and fun loving; in short, he was an easy interview and his cooking was new, chic, exciting and exotic for its time. As word of blackened redfish spread across the country, several phenomena occurred. Blackened foods started appearing on menus all over the country with mixed results, Gulf of Mexico redfish (actually a specimen of the drum genus) was overfished to the brink of species extinction, and the lines of people waiting for a seat at K-Paul's and hoping for a glimpse of its suddenly superstar chef stretched down Chartres Street before turning the corner and continuing on Conti.

Prudhomme's staff, mostly family in the restaurant's earliest days, shared the larger-than-life chef's joie de vivre and playful nature, applying stick-on foil stars to customers' faces, the star's color being determined by how clean a customer's plate was once he or she pushed back from the table. The Sensible One was vastly amused by Prudhomme's "star system," reattaching her collection of stars to her driver's license. Her sense of humor, however, wasn't fully appreciated by the state trooper brandishing a radar gun and ticket pad.

Despite the overflowing plates of a new American fusion cuisine and the joy with which it was served, a considerable number of condescending residents dismissed K-Paul's as "okay for tourists" and stayed away. In the midst of runaway success, Prudhomme was in danger of becoming its victim. But instead of growing alarmed by the situation, America's hottest chef considered it an opportunity to grow his flourishing business.

Fifteen years ago, the restaurant expanded its capacity to 200 people on two floors, a balcony and a courtyard, resulting in revived favor with the city's local diners. Business is still booming and most people know it would be foolhardy trying to get a table without making a reservation.

It's difficult to believe that K-Paul's is now over thirty years old, and perhaps even more difficult to believe that Prudhomme himself is over seventy. Although he no longer cooks for customers in the restaurant at 416 Chartres Street, having turned over Executive Chef duties to Paul Miller some years ago, his presence remains regular and, even on those occasions when he's not on the premises, palpable.

In the wake of Katrina's destruction, Prudhomme was adamant about K-Paul's Louisiana Kitchen being one of the first French Quarter restaurants to reopen for business. Knowing that the city's community of musicians was hit just as hard as the restaurant industry, Prudhomme hired jazz musicians to play on the sidewalk at his front door, a practice that still occurs from time to time, now years after the fact.

Over the past quarter century, Prudhomme's circle of operations has expanded. Samples of spices requested by early customers grew into Magic Seasonings Blends®, a spice and sauces company doing business in all 50 states and more than two dozen nations. His first cookbook, *Chef Paul Prudhomme's Louisiana Kitchen*, is nearing its 100th printing and has been followed by eight more books. Despite the spice blends, books, television enterprises and image/brand licensing, the true wellspring of the empire continues to come out of the Chartres Street kitchen six nights a week.

It may be misleading to say the cuisine has developed over the past thirty years; the more appropriate word is probably "refined." While the relatively short menu is rewritten daily to both reflect and take advantage of the seasonal and regional offerings that give Prudhomme's signature brand of Louisiana cooking its identity, there are always a few basics to be found.

Of course, there is a blackened fish, although these days it's far more likely to be a black drum than a classic redfish. From time to time, a "bronzed" fish (or other meat), the result of less heat and peppers, appears on the menu. While tamer than their blackened cousins, these dishes are still probably too intense for people gauche enough to ask their waitperson, "Is it spicy?" On that note, most of the food coming out of the Prudhomme/Miller kitchen can certainly be considered to be "full-flavored" if not out-and-out spicy, and those with nervous stomachs or overly delicate digestive systems should really consider going somewhere else and leave the hard-to-get seats for those who will truly appreciate them.

The kitchen notably turns out magnificent etouffées, the "smothered" stews of seafood or chicken cooked with the "trinity" (celery, green pepper and onion) in a smoky roux and served around a scoop of rice.

Prudhomme has been known to say that, "Everyone in South Louisiana makes their own special gumbo – and they are all fantastic." While I'm inclined to disagree, having tasted a few that most assuredly fall short of Chef Paul's level of enthusiasm, it would certainly be an injustice not to highlight the chef's own rendering of what amounts to the national dish of Louisiana. It is rich, smoky and twice as filling as it looks sitting so innocently in a cup.

Interestingly enough, Prudhomme enjoys his gumbo with a scoop of potato salad in it. Figuring "If that's how the master eats it, I'll give it a shot," I did. It was, well, interesting, but not enough for me to make a habit of it, particularly when both elements are wonderful on their own.

Prices at K-Paul's strike some people I know as high, the impression I initially had – at least until my first forkful. At that very moment, any correlation between a handful of nickels and a single bite of manna became sheer folly.

Money isn't really the point at K-Paul's Louisiana Kitchen, and perhaps it never has been. For over a generation, Paul Prudhomme has been more than a chef, spice merchant and cheerleader for a city recovering from the largest disaster in our national history. He's been a true American culinary icon, a Louisiana answer to Frances' Paul Bocuse and Auguste Escoffier, as well as the successor to Julia Child and the acknowledged trailblazer for what has become New Orleans' Golden Age of Chefs.

And how does anyone put a price tag on a national treasure?

K-Paul's Louisiana Kitchen
Louisiana Fusion
419 Chartres Street
(Between Conti and St. Louis Streets)
0.3 miles by foot from The Zero Point
Lunch served Tuesday through Saturday,
11:00 a.m. to 2:00 p.m.
Dinner served Monday through Saturday,
5:30 p.m. to 10:00 p.m.
All major credit cards are honored and
reservations emphatically recommended
To make a reservation, call at 504-596-2530
between 10 a.m. and 8 p.m. CST,
or visit the online reservation service
Cell phones are not allowed in any of the dining rooms
Website: www.chefpaul.com

Bayona

*If history serves as any guide, expect further changes
in Bayona's menus to reflect the new discoveries Spicer makes
in her constantly evolving whirlwind of a life.*

FOR WELL OVER TWENTY YEARS, I have been unsuccessfully
trying to describe Susan Spicer, the celebrated owner/chef
of Bayona in the French Quarter – and that's precisely how
I've described her. It's as futile as trying to describe a
chameleon by using only one color.

The problem is, just when I think I have her pegged, she
changes and what was once a concise assessment is hopelessly out of date. This has been going on for almost a quarter century, during which I have been regally fed in her
restaurants, charmed during our brief howdy-shakes when
she makes her rounds, and exasperated when I've tried and
failed to replicate her signature pepper jelly glazed duck
breast in my own kitchen, armed with her recipe but hand-
icapped by my personal shortage of talent.

Not terribly long ago, I was looking for something to
cook and started thumbing through her superb *Crescent
City Cooking*, a cookbook I thought was never going to
come out. In her opening paragraph, she reminisces about
a warm spring evening in 1979 when she walked in front
of the restaurant on Dauphine Street that would ulti-

mately become Bayona. She was on her way to her first cooking job.

I couldn't help but wonder if I was sitting in the restaurant that evening. The restaurant was Maison Pierre, where Cajun / French chef Pierre Lacoste was making a big noise putting out classic French food with Louisiana ingredients. I remember the place as being appropriately fussy and French, but not much else beyond it being the first restaurant where I ever saw a $5,000 bottle on the wine list. (I asked the waiter if anyone had ever bought one and he imperiously told me that the house had sold two – to the same table in one evening -- to two Texans celebrating a rather substantial oil strike.)

Spicer's rise through the kitchen ranks was rapid. In 1986, after a couple of stints in New Orleans and Paris, some extensive traveling and a first executive chef gig at a now defunct restaurant called Savoir Faire, she opened the 40-seat Bistro at Maison de Ville, the French Quarter gem of a hotel where Tennessee Williams is said to have drafted the greater part of A Streetcar Named Desire. To a kitchen so small it included only one oven, four burners and a refrigerator in the alley, Spicer brought her seven short years of experience to a city with a centuries old reputation as one of America's centers of fine cuisine.

From that point forward, it's been pretty much a Cinderella story for Spicer, minus the cruel stepmother, the glass slipper and the coach that turned into a pumpkin at the stroke of midnight.

The Bistro at Maison de Ville was a success from the beginning, and it was there where Spicer developed such signature dishes as her Cream of Garlic Soup, Grilled Shrimp with Black Bean Cakes and her Seared Duck Breast with Pepper Jelly Glaze. Through the pass-through window opening up to the postage stamp of a kitchen, Chef Spicer could watch people react to the food, which helped her refine current dishes and fine-tune new ones.

It was during her years at Maison De Ville when her original cooking (which she dubbed "New World" cuisine) was wrongly labeled as nouvelle cuisine and she became falsely typecast as a practitioner of nouvelle (which was once described by a comedian as "I just paid $94 for what?"). This was at a time when nouvelle cuisine was the darling of New York culinary / media circles, and almost any type of cooking using an unusual ingredient was hailed as an innovative example.

Despite the runaway success of both the cuisine and Spicer's reputation, the Bistro at Maison de Ville was owned by the hotel, and entrepreneurial fires were beginning to burn in its headline chef. One of Spicer's regular customers, Regina Keever offered to back her in a restaurant of her own, and on April Fool's night of 1990, the building which had once housed Maison Pierre opened its doors as Bayona, which was the name of Dauphine Street when New Orleans was under its original Spanish rule. It had been ten-and-one-half years since Susan Spicer admired the building on the way to her first kitchen job.

With a ready-built fan base from her years at the Bistro, a site that had already serve as a showcase for one headline chef, and Chef Spicer's penchant for experimentation and invention, it took little time for Bayona to grow into one of

New Orleans' most beloved restaurants. Its reputation was cemented when Spicer was named "Best Chef, Southeast" in the 1993 James Beard Awards, the top accolades in the American restaurant industry. By this time, Chef Spicer had become a permanent fixture in discussions of the city's new guard of chefs along with Frank Brigtsen, Emeril Lagasse and other rising stars opening their own restaurants within a few years of each other.

Despite Spicer's success and the attention paid to her cuisine, a clear label for it remained elusive. The "New World" designation gained some traction, but no one could adequately say what it meant. Due to the excesses of self-promoting chefs more concerned with an ingredient's eccentricity than its flavor, the nouvelle cuisine moniker was losing its cachet. Complicating the process was the fact that Spicer was (and remains) an inveterate tinkerer whose cuisine kept evolving as she continued learning.

And perhaps that's the most appropriate name for Spicer's style of cooking – evolutionary. With life changes come cooking changes. Her later in life marriage and instant family of two children started bringing elements of traditional "home cooking" more to the forefront in her recipe development.

Through her collaboration with former partner Donald Link in their very successful restaurant Herbsaint, a new depth and rusticity came into her repertoire. In 2010, she opened another new restaurant, Mondo, in New Orleans' Lakeview neighborhood as a casual alternative to the more formal Bayona. If history serves as any guide, expect further changes in Bayona's menus to reflect the new discoveries

Spicer makes in her constantly evolving whirlwind of a life.

A look at the Bayona menu, which changes regularly to take advantage of the seasonal freshness of regionally produced ingredients, and her cookbook gives me the impression that, in most cases, Louisiana is the source of a recipe's central ingredient and the rest of the world is her spice cabinet. This can be found in such dishes as Indian-spiced Turkey Breast with Creamy Red Lentils, Mediterranean Roasted Shrimp with Crispy Risotto Cakes or Shrimp Salad with Fennel and Herbed Cream Cheese on Brioche.

There's also a playful side to Spicer, one of whose most often ordered lunch items is Smoked Duck "PBJ" with Cashew Butter, Pepper Jelly and Apple-Celery Salad, a gourmet take on the old favorite childhood finger food.

Both Bayona's lunch and dinner menus always feature several of the chef's established signature dishes, and fresh-from-market items that have been the beneficiaries of Spicer's dazzling technical skills, intuitiveness and imagination.

The three smallish rooms and the private patio of the 200 year-old Creole cottage that house Bayona are conducive to civilized conversation without being stuffy. With apricot walls and a profusion of flowers, the white tablecloth restaurant has a formal look, but an unexpectedly informal feel to it. It is not uncommon, late in the evening shift when the kitchen becomes less frenetic, to see Spicer talking to customers and collecting opinions or enjoying a glass of white wine with old friends. Despite the fact that she now has a chef de cuisine overseeing the day-to-day operation of the kitchen, the restaurant is very much "home" to Susan Spicer, and she goes out of her way to make you feel like it's yours as well.

After twenty years of success, the very notion of failure at Bayona is dismissed as preposterous, at least for as long as its energetic chef stays at the helm. But watching Susan Spicer work, as I have since her earliest days at the Bistro at Maison de Ville, one gets the feeling that at least one of her eyes will remain as open to future opportunity as her heart has always been.

For the time being, at least, it's business as usual at Bayona, and business is booming. As for tomorrow or next week or next year, who knows? It's a constantly changing world for Chef Spicer, but there's one thing you can be sure of: If you want a seat at one of her tables, you might want to make reservations several weeks in advance. Because time waits for nobody.

Bayona
New World Evolutionary
430 Dauphine Street (between Conti and St. Louis Streets)
0.4 miles from The Zero Point
Lunch served Wednesday through Saturday from 11:30 a.m.
Dinner served Monday through Saturday from 6:00 p.m.
Dark on Sunday
All major credit cards accepted and reservations are essential
Telephone: (504) 525-4455
Website: www.bayona.com

Herbsaint

The shrimp was, quite simply, a revelation – still tender and
carrying a taste that made me dream of salt air and tall ships,
but prominently balanced among the vibrant flavors
combined around it. In truth, I have never had better.

HOW CAN YOU HELP but like stories of people who have boot-strapped their way from the bottom to the top? Case in point: Donald Link, the proprietor and executive chef of Herbsaint, the Louisiana bistro with a decidedly French accent.

A truly local talent, Link's culinary career started at age fifteen washing dishes and scrubbing pots in a cramped restaurant scullery. In a story with so many Horatio Alger overtones that no self-respecting Hollywood producer would ever think of filming it, Link kicked around New Orleans kitchens, picking up a trick here and a technique there until he had learned enough skills to start developing a reputation of his own.

In 1993, he headed west to San Francisco, where he attended the Culinary Institute of America and started broadening his horizons in Bay Area restaurants. He returned to New Orleans in 1995, lured by the opportunity to work with Susan Spicer, whose five-year-old French Quarter restaurant, Bayona, was already one of the city's most celebrated places to dine.

After a two-year stint that saw him rise to sous chef at Bayona, Link returned to the Bay Area, working for three more years before once again returning to New Orleans for the opportunity that would make the Crescent City his permanent home. Working with Spicer again, but this time as collaborator and partner, he opened Herbsaint near the heart of New Orleans' Central Business District (CBD).

Within a few years, Spicer left the Herbsaint kitchen and refocused her energies on Bayona, a new cookbook and a less formal restaurant in the city's Lakeview section. Link continued keeping Herbsaint on track and also expanded his circle of operations to include a stylish new restaurant named Cochon (French for "pig") with an accompanying charcuterie.

Were this indeed a Horatio Alger story, years of hard work, gumption and pluck would have followed and Herbsaint would have slowly grown into a beloved mainstay of the New Orleans restaurant scene. The truth is, Herbsaint was an overnight sensation, that is, if it took that long at all. While no one will ever mistake Herbsaint for one of the grand palaces of haute cuisine New Orleans style, there exists a natural synchronicity between the city and the bistro that is undeniable.

Should you stand across the street and look at Herbsaint, it looks as if someone scattered some tables and chairs in front of a prepossessing, utilitarian building. But as you look longer, you'll notice the tables have white linen tablecloths, while the building has a small gallery and sits behind a stand of leafy trees. The thought that someone might have lifted the whole street corner from a Paris backstreet is almost un-avoidable. But every few minutes, the rumble and clatter of an aged green streetcar rolling down historic St. Charles Avenue serves to remind you that you could only be in one American city, and it is "the city that care forgot."

Should you choose to dine inside, Herbsaint is a decidedly understated room. There are some postmodern light fixtures interspersed along the walls that keep the room from feeling blank. A screened fabric depicting tuxedoed jazz musicians subtly blends into the large wall at the back end of the dining room. The bar itself is small and tucked into a corner of the main room, out of traffic, and making the place's appellation as a "bar and restaurant" seem reversed. Whether by accident or intent, there is a feeling that the room itself is understated so as not to detract from the main event, which is most assuredly the food.

Like the physical restaurant itself, Herbsaint's cuisine seems to have one foot in France and its other in Louisiana. This is not surprising, considering that both Spicer and Link spent the bulk of their formative years in New Orleans and had the early parts of their careers shaped in restaurants with pronounced Gallic influences. The result is a fusion that is at once local and global, contemporary but with a classical pedigree. Although it has been a number of years since Spicer's departure, the plates at Herbsaint still reflect the natural collaboration of two chefs with comparable backgrounds yet divergent points of view.

The menus for both lunch and dinner are relatively short, with each offering less than a dozen small plates and main courses in addition to soups, salads and sides. These are complemented by two or three off-menu specials that appear to revolve around seasonal specialties.

The language of the menus is both spare and matter of fact, adding an air of elegant simplicity to the cuisine itself. With such offerings as "sautéed Louisiana jumbo shrimp with mushrooms, bacon and spoon bread" and "Muscovy duck leg confit with dirty rice and citrus gastrique," adjectives designed to rouse an appetite would seem not only superfluous, but downright silly.

About the only place the simplicity of the menu language fails is the "antipasto plate" located on the small plates section of the dinner menu. When I ordered it without asking what items or ingredients were included, I had done so with the suspicion it might contain a morsel or two from Link's charcuterie at Cochon, duly famous for using "every part of the pig except the squeal." Once it arrived, the waiter pointed out each item and explained what it was so rapidly that my memory could not absorb, let alone retain the inventory. To my delight, I was served what effectively amounted to a sampling platter from Cochon, containing a petite ramekin of a rabbit terrine, a pâté, shaved slices of a hard sausage and three or four other items with names I can't recall, but the flavors of which I'll not soon forget.

The antipasto plate was an effective curtain-raiser for the Muscovy Duck, which had a deep, smoky flavor evocative of Cajun country, an effect that was amplified by combining the duck with dirty rice, the regional specialty cooked with chicken livers and gizzards, onion, peppers and garlic. The citrus gastrique glazing the duck, a reduction of caramelized sugar and oranges, finished the dish with an inspired whisper of French culinary classicism.

The Sensible One (who has a knack for ordering what I really wanted but didn't know it) opted for a simple green salad, followed by a shrimp risotto with capers in a buttery sauce. The shrimp was, quite simply, a revelation -- still tender and carrying a taste that made me dream of salt air and tall ships, but prominently balanced among the vibrant flavors combined around it. In truth, I have never had better.

If anything, balance seems to be the watchword at Herbsaint. From its beginning in 2000, the restaurant has appeared to have effortlessly balanced the culinary classicism of La Belle France with the Cajun and Creole cooking traditions of New Orleans. Herbsaint's exceptional owner/chef Donald Link has balanced the pressures of maintaining the standards not only of such an extraordinary restaurant, but also of Cochon, its accompanying charcuterie and a private dining facility, Calcasieu, named for the Louisiana parish in which he grew up. In the process, he was named a James Beard Award winner for both his work in the kitchen (Best Chef: Southeast, 2007) and as the author of *Real Cajun: Rustic Home Cooking from Donald Link's Louisiana* (Best Cookbook, 2009).

Horatio Alger would be mighty proud.

Herbsaint Bar and Restaurant
French-inspired Louisiana
0.4 miles from The Zero Point
701 St. Charles (at Girod Street)
Lunch served Monday-Friday 11:30 a.m. – 1:30 p.m.
Dinner served Monday-Saturday 5:30 p.m. – 10:00 p.m.
BISTRO open Monday-Friday 1:30 – 5:30 p.m.
All major credit cards accepted
and reservations are strongly advised
Telephone: (504) 524-4114
Website: www.herbsaint.com

Mandina's

At some point in time, someone must have walked out of
Mandina's looking for more food – perhaps a sumo wrestler
or a lumberjack coming off a three-day fast.

THE IDEA OF OPENING a restaurant was the furthest thing
from Sebastian Mandina's mind.

It was 1898, the threshold of a new, twentieth century, and
Mandina had emigrated from Palermo, Sicily, to New Or-
leans in order to open a corner grocery in the growing Mid-
City area. With his family settled in upstairs, he opened his
store and started chipping off his piece of the American
Dream.

Over time, the grocery evolved into a pool hall that sold
sandwiches and the business was handed down to the two
sons who continued to live above the store. By 1932, the
Great Depression had arrived and Frank and Anthony Mandina decided their financial future would be more secure if
it depended upon serving full meals to families instead of
sandwiches to shooters and sharks. It was an idea that made
sense for the times.

It still makes perfect sense today, as evidenced by the
lines waiting for tables in the same building on the corner
of Canal and Cortez Streets, where the same family (albeit
several generations downstream) dishes out their now

time-honored Creole-Italian brand of New Orleans home cooking.

Mandina's has been self-described as "the quintessential New Orleans neighborhood restaurant," and few would disagree. With its pedigree including a groceria and a pool-room, Mandina's makes no pretense of being anything other than what it is: namely, a place that has continually evolved into what New Orleanians want it to be instead of a high-flying innovator hoping the city may follow its lead.

Beyond a modicum of kitchen modernizing and gussying up the bar and dining rooms after Hurricane Katrina poured three feet of water in the door, little has changed. The food is the same, the atmosphere is equally comfortable and the family went out of its way to make sure the faces throughout the operation remained the same.

Walking into Mandina's for the first or fiftieth time is an exercise in sudden comfort. The room and the bar area are nice enough, yet pleasantly informal. Large windows look through neon onto one of the quieter stretches of Canal Street, where red streetcars rumble by on a regular basis. Framed JazzFest posters adorn the walls, occasionally interspersed with old photographs. There are no booths, only tables and chairs. With its high ceilings, the room levels ambient noise into an even, yet lively buzz.

The room is a natural showcase of democracy having dinner. It is not uncommon to see a table of businessmen having a martini before lunch next to a table of blue-jeaned inhabitants from the surrounding neighborhoods to three generations of a family celebrating Grandma's birthday to a couple on a first date. The amount of people watching seems minimal, most people appearing absorbed in negotiating their way through very generous plates of food.

At some point in time, someone must have walked out of Mandina's looking for more food – perhaps a sumo wrestler or a lumberjack coming off a three-day fast. For mere mortals, however, most portions of most items are large enough to share, and the rest are even bigger.

Consider starting with the onion rings. An "appetizer" portion is served on a platter that will easily feed four as a starter (and a "side" of French fries is even larger). The rings themselves show years of patron pleasing experience in the kitchen; they're thin enough not to be daunting, but not so thin that they droop or break the moment they're picked up. On a recent visit, our server was kind enough to ask The Sensible One and me if we'd like a half order, something that doesn't appear on the menu or we even knew existed. "No, go ahead and give us a regular order," we said. Foolishly.

I used to believe I always ordered Mandina's homemade turtle soup au sherry as a matter of habit, until I realized it had actually become a ritual. Watch the soup arrive at the table. Wait for the server to ask if I'd like a little more sherry and wait for the bottle to be instantly produced. Say "please." Smile as the server adds somewhere between a dash and a dollop to give it some wallop. Dig in, knowing all is right in the world for the next few minutes, anyway.

Over the years, turtle soup has changed, much like New Orleans itself. Originally made from sea turtles weighing up to 1,000 pounds, ecological and conservation considerations have caused many turtle soup chefs to specify smaller, fresh-water specimens, which numerous people believe has a gamier, brackish taste. This flavor is sometimes smoothed out through the addition or substitution of other meats, normally veal or pork, in the soup's preparation. In some instances, the substitution is terrapin, a smaller, East Coast turtle with a taste some epicures proclaim superior.

Turtle soup is a polarizing dish. It seems that no one greets it with indifference; they love it or loathe it. The soup appears on numerous menus throughout the city, but New Orleans partisans will almost always include Mandina's and one of the Brennan family outposts (usually Commander's Palace or their eponymous French Quarter flagship) among their top two or three favorites. For visitors unfamiliar with classic Crescent City preparations of turtle soup, Mandina's is a very good place to get a first taste.

For a city of big, wide ranging appetites, Mandina's menu has expanded to fit them all. Steaks, chops, chicken, seafood, soups, salads, and sides join a variety of Italian, daily and house specials along with a list of burgers, a muffuletta and poor boys that hearken back to the restaurant's earlier life as a pool hall.

While such a wide selection can be confusing, even intimidating, the real heart of Mandina's menu is to be found in its House Specials section, a half dozen seafood entrees that are the foundation of the restaurant's venerable popularity. Among them are speckled trout, fresh catfish from legendary Bayou Des Allemands and seasonal soft shell crabs, all prepared in the classically simple New Orleans Meuniere or Almandine styles. But if there is one special that truly blends the city's Creole and Italian culinary cultures, it's the

Gilled Shrimp over Pasta Bordelaise.

"Bordelaise" New Orleans style should not be confused with the Bordeaux district in France or the rich white or brown sauces laden with shallots and herbs that bear the same name. In New Orleans, Bordelaise can be translated to "garlic, butter, garlic, leaf parsley, garlic, occasional thyme and, oh yeah, garlic." The dish is the essence of simplicity itself. Plump, fresh Louisiana shrimp are grilled before being dumped atop a mountain of pasta drenched in this buttery, garlicky sauce. The portion size is enormous to the point The Sensible One and I normally split an order and still leave some on the platter. In the dish's sheer simplicity, every flavor comes through in an inspired blend. Yes, there's enough garlic that you'll want to take a roll of breath mints. Hell, you might think of taking two, but this is old style New Orleans Italian cooking at its best and most generous.

Mandina's is anything but tony, hip or au courant. It's a working class family restaurant that's been catering to local tastes instead of creating them for three quarters of a century.

And boy, does it work.

One final note: Unless you show up a few minutes before the doors open or prefer to dine in the middle of the afternoon, you should expect to wait for a table, particularly on weekends. Reservations aren't accepted for parties of less than six, and credit cards aren't accepted at all. Should you find this way of doing business particularly old-fashioned, you may want to tell a member of the family. He or she will no doubt thank you for it.

Mandina's Restaurant
Creole Italian
1.8 by car miles from The Zero Point
3800 Canal St (at South Cortez)
Open Monday – Thursday, 11:00 a.m. - 9:30 p.m.
Friday & Saturday 11:00 a.m., 10:00 p.m.
Sunday, Noon – 9:00 p.m.
Cash only, no credit cards or
reservations for less than six are accepted
Telephone: 504-482-9179
Website: www.mandinasrestaurant.com

Parkway Bakery and Tavern

An unadorned frame building sitting on a corner in a tattered section of the city, it is at once a neighborhood landmark and a wistful reminder of better days behind.

THE GREATER NEW ORLEANS AREA is home to roughly one million people, about one million of whom are restaurant and food critics. Were it possible to get 1,000,000 New Orleanians organized for anything, arguing the merits of restaurants and their fare would be the city's official sport.

This is particularly true about poor boys – the sandwich you might know by the names hero, submarine, gyro, torpedo, grinder or any number of others. Hell, they can't even agree on what to properly call the sandwiches. Some ersatz historians insist they are "poor boys," while other choose the more colloquial shorthand of "po'boy."

About the only thing poor boy purists can agree upon is that if it isn't made with New Orleans style French bread, it isn't a poor boy.

While poor boys can be found everywhere from white tablecloth places to corner grocery stores, natives generally seem to favor taverns or small cafes that run from tidy Mom-and-Pops to corner bars that can be called colorful, if not downright scruffy. One thing they all have in common is that their devotees are passionate.

Fans of the roast beef poor boy at Parasol's will never concede that a better version may be found at Domilise's since both have been featured on Travel Network series. Those who prefer their poor boys stuffed with buttery New Orleans style barbecue shrimp will square off between Liuzza's-by-the-Track and the original lunch special at Pascal's Manale. French Quarter residents and visitors alike have chosen between Johnny's and Café Maspero for decades.

A comparative newcomer to the battle is Crabby Jack's, a small cafe in front of a commercial seafood market, known for such unusual ingredients as crisp fried calamari and a slow-roasted duck in its own gravy. And fans of oysters, freshly shucked, battered and plunged in oil still bemoan the fact that Gail and Anthony Uglesich never reopened their rickety, ten-table restaurant after Hurricane Katrina and the ultimate oyster poor boy has faded into memory.

Beyond the eight establishments mentioned above, there are scores of places in every corner of the city offering their take on ingredients classical or creative, and each has its own retinue of die-hard supporters.

Trying to name a best poor boy or place to buy one would be a fool's errand at best, and incitement to fisticuffs at worst. That said, people with enough time to visit just one poor boy place on short visits to the city would do well to consider Parkway Bakery and Tavern in the Mid-City, a short block off Bayou St. John. One such one-timer was President Obama, who brought along the family and half the Secret Service.

With a history traceable back to 1913, Parkway is the very embodiment of old New Orleans neighborhood places. An unadorned frame building sitting on a corner in a tattered section of the city, it is at once a neighborhood landmark and a wistful reminder of better days behind. The place had been boarded up before a local entrepreneur restored and reopened it in the early 2000s before it had to be redone a second time in Katrina's aftermath.

There is an essential honesty about Parkway that "is what it is" without pretense or affectation. The front room is a small bar, the back room is a utilitarian sandwich café, and outside there is a covered deck and patio, where bands sometimes play on weekends or the spontaneous, informal holidays that seem so often to spring up on the New Orleans calendar. The decor is mainly old signs and pieces of Saints memorabilia.

The sandwiches come to your table or barstool wrapped in white butcher paper. Napkins are in a dispenser along with salt, pepper and New Orleans-made Crystal Hot Sauce wrapped in a Parkway label. The wait staff is young and cheerful.

In such prosaic, workmanlike surroundings, everything succeeds or fails on the quality of the food, and in that sense, Parkway is an unconditional success. While eavesdropping suggests that the dressed roast beef and fried seafood poor boys are the runaway favorites, visual reconnaissance shows people diving into the spectrum of Parkway's offerings with no visible indicators of the least discontent.

The menu lists nineteen poor boys in either regular (eight-inch) or large (twelve-inch) sizes, a grilled cheese on white or wheat and a grilled Reuben on rye. A good many of them are traditional and predictable (ham, turkey, marinara meatball, chicken breast, various sausages and the like). Some are indigenous to the city.

New Orleans roast beef is slow-cooked in a gravy that's thicker than that generally found in Chicago Italian beef or French dip sandwiches. Once "dressed," New Orleans patois for lettuce, tomatoes and mayonnaise (pronounced "my-nez") with pickles, onions and Zatarain's Creole mustard optional, there is usually little way to contain all the ingredients in the flaky crust and airy centered French bread in which the conglomeration is assembled. Oh, hell, let's just call it what it is; it's a mess, but a mighty fine one.

Because of New Orleans' gulf location, fresh seafood is abundant, making fried shrimp and oyster poor boys the other main entries in the Parkway repertoire. During their short season, the restaurant occasionally lists soft shell crab poor boys as blackboard specials. For those with larger appetites (and a handy change of clothes), Parkway offers its own Surf'N'Turf, a combination of roast beef, gravy and fried shrimp.

Beyond the traditional standards, Parkway has a gravy only poor boy on the menu, as well as one made with French fried potatoes where one would expect to find meat. This has progressed, of course, into the fully dressed, gravy-slathered, French fries poor boy. In a nod to Louisiana's Cajun heritage, the restaurant also lists an alligator sausage poor boy on its lengthy menu.

While Parkway has full bar service, a look at the tables will show most of them covered with frosty beer bottles or longnecks of Barq's root beer, a regional favorite long before it was purchased by the Coca-Cola Company, and the traditional accompaniment for a classic New Orleans poor boy.

On a side note, while no one is absolutely certain of the origin of the term "poor boy," the most commonly bandied about explanation is that it goes back to a four-month 1929 streetcar strike in New Orleans. Legend has it that restaurateur Clovis Martin, who had formerly been a streetcar conductor, offered free sandwiches to striking workers. The restaurant workers would joke, "here comes another poor boy," and the name was soon stuck on the sandwiches.

Some people may – and some people will – take issue with the selection of Parkway Bakery and Tavern as a solid representative of the hundreds of poor boy places in New Orleans and the surrounding areas. The argument will last forever, and there will never be a definite winner declared.

So try this. Ask a cabbie where to get the best poor boy in the city. Ask a bartender or a cop or a construction worker. Then go there. But make sure you have a lot of napkins handy.

Parkway Bakery and Tavern
Poor boys
2.4 miles from The Zero Point
539 Hagan Avenue (at the corner of Toulouse)
Open 11:00 a.m. until 10:00 p.m.
Wednesday through Monday
All major credit cards are accepted
Telephone: (504) 482-3047
Website: www.parkwaybakeryandtavernnola.com

Casamento's

*A typical dozen will usually contain both smaller oysters
with their intense flavor and some so large
you'll suspect that if they ever produced pearls,
they'd be large enough to play golf with.*

THE DIFFERENCE BETWEEN TWO of New Orleans' most
venerated and revered oyster bars can be summarized in
one simple sentence:

Casamento's is for purists, and the Acme is for tourists.

While such a statement may seem pejorative at face
value, it is not a knock on the food served at either establishment, since most New Orleanians would put both places
in the city's top five classic oyster bars.

The differences between the two are to be found in
the addresses and attitudes toward change. The Acme is
located in the tourist end of the upper French Quarter,
between Bourbon and Royal Streets, while Casamento's
can be found near the corner of Napoleon and Magazine
in a more genteel residential and shopping district.

In the last fifteen years, Acme has opened four new
satellite locations, including one in Destin (Florida), while
Casamento's has stayed in the twenty-foot wide storefront
where they opened their doors in 1919.

When sushi was all the rage in the early 1990s, Acme

tossed some scallions and wasabi on their raw oysters and touted them as "Cajun Sushi." When another New Orleans restaurant, Drago's, developed the charbroiled oysters that took the city by storm, "chargrilled oysters" quickly appeared on the Acme menu. By contrast, Casamento's has stuck with the oyster basics – on the half shell, fried and oyster stew – and watched the fads pass by their doorstep.

Whether Casamento's dogged resistance to change has been created by over 90 years of success or plain old hardheadedness on the part of the owners is difficult to say, but the bottom line is, it works well for them.

On the history page of the restaurant's website is a photograph of the front room taken in 1919. With the exception of the tiles on the counter front, a few different pictures on the walls and some updated equipment, it is nearly identical to the view you get when you first walk in the door. That sameness extends into the second dining room behind as well.

While there's no way of knowing if Italian immigrant Joe Casamento could envision a ninety year run for his restaurant, one of his key early decisions has made it possible for the place to make very few changes as the decades have danced by. Following restaurant traditions of his native Italy, Casamento had tiles installed on all the floors and walls to make the restaurant easy to clean. In fact, so many tiles were ordered for the restaurant's initial installation that it took four separate tile companies from across the United States to fulfill the order.

This selfsame order of tile still covers the floor and lower ten feet of walls today, and the place remains spotless. Original tile also surrounds the twin picture windows, front door and transoms, giving Casamento's storefront façade its frozen-in-time quality.

While such timeless visual elements enhance both Casamento's aesthetics and charm, it's not the architecture or décor that's served on the plate. It's the food in general and the oysters in particular.

Should you arrive for an early lunch before the doors open at eleven, the chances are fairly good that you'll be met with the reassuring sight of men with burlap bags on their shoulders delivering the day's freshly caught oysters. If you're seated in the front room and take the opportunity to watch the speed and sure-handedness with which the shuckers work, you'll realize that not only did you arrive for lunch before your lunch ever showed up, but the whole process happened in a number of minutes you can count on your fingers.

It is at this point where visitors from outside the Gulf of Mexico's main oystering centers (running from Abbeville, Louisiana, to Apalachicola, Florida) come face to face with a conflict raging between coastal seafood harvesters and overreaching federal bureaucrats hell-bent on creating a "nanny state." At the center of the controversy is if and to what degree eating raw oysters can be potentially dangerous to human health.

For nearly twenty years, a disclaimer has appeared on menus in most oyster bars warning of health hazards associated with eating raw shellfish. The reason for the somewhat disconcerting warning is *Vibrio vulnificus*, a bacterium that naturally occurs in some oysters. While nothing in this essay should be construed as a professional medical opinion (yes, we writers have to put down disclaimers, too), a combination of facts, history and common sense suggests that the vast majority of the populace have little to nothing to fear from consuming raw oysters.

The truth is, people with serious pre-existing health conditions, such as liver disease, cancer, diabetes, AIDS or other autoimmunity problems, account for virtually all illnesses and deaths (about fifteen per year) from raw oyster consumption. Actuarial figures suggest that a person is far more likely to die from a lightning strike than seafood consumption. Nonetheless, people with conditions putting them at risk are advised to only eat oysters that have been cooked, frozen or pasteurized – a recommendation that already appears on many oyster bar menus. (In fact, Casamento's menu contains: "Warning: There may be a risk associated with consuming raw shellfish as is the case with other raw protein products. If you suffer from chronic illness of the liver, stomach, or blood, or have other immune disorders, you should eat these products fully cooked.")

Despite the odds against any harm from eating raw oysters, in the fall of 2009, the United States Food & Drug Administration issued a plan to prohibit the sale of raw Gulf Coast oysters for six or more months per year, starting in 2011. The proposed ban was fought by the coastal seafood and oyster industries, which stood to lose thousands of jobs should the proposal be enacted, before a compromise resolution was drafted late in 2011 and sent to Congress for passage.

That said, the oysters on the half shell at Casamento's are magnificent. A typical dozen will usually contain both smaller oysters with their intense flavor and some so large you'll suspect that if they ever produced pearls, they'd be large enough to play golf with.

Fried oysters and shrimp are available as dinners or as "boats," which are not traditional New Orleans poor boys, but overflowing sandwiches made with the equivalent of Texas toast. Catfish, trout and seasonal soft-shell crabs are also available in both configurations.

The pocket-sized kitchen also produces chicken tenders, spaghetti and meatballs and a seafood combo platter, while a gumbo pot simmers and their overworked fryers produce a steady stream of crab claw and calamari plates.

While there are any number of places to grab a great dozen or two on the half shell in New Orleans, there is an old-fashioned, turn-back-the-clock quality about Casamento's that separates it from the pack. Perhaps the restaurant being closed every June, July and August best illustrates this. Years ago, oysters were traditionally served in months with an "R" in their spellings. While it's true that summer months are not the best for mollusk harvesting, improved oystering techniques have made the "R" rule more of a myth than anything else. That doesn't mean you won't see some sort of plaque reading, "Oysters 'R' in Season" in oyster bars all across America, although I've never noticed one in Casamento's.

Even though the restaurant stays open through the "R-less" month of May, there remains a charm to its contrarian adherence to myth. And it's that devotion to times past which makes Casamento's the Crescent City's quintessential oyster house, at least for purists.

Casamento's Restaurant
Oysters
3.3 miles from The Zero Point
4330 Magazine St. (at Napoleon)
Open Tuesday - Saturday from 11:00 a.m. - 2:00 p.m.
Thursdays, Fridays and Saturday Evenings
from 5:30 p.m. - 9:00 p.m.
Closed June, July and August and all major holidays
Casamento's accepts cash only and no reservations
Telephone: 504-895-9761
Website: www. casamentosrestaurant.com

Brigtsen's

It is "Next Step Louisiana Cuisine,"
its Cajun and Creole heritages unmistakable,
but without the preciousness or over-the-top eccentricities
of nouvelle cuisine's outer reaches.

PERHAPS IT'S A REFLECTION on our society's celebrity obsession, or maybe it's the number of media outlets that need to keep their fires stoked around the clock, but the true currency of celebrity has been devalued by the increasing number of people who find themselves so pronounced by a fickle public and the breathless media that panders to them.

It's only natural that in a city like New Orleans, where food outstrips even the weather as the leading topic of discussion, chefs would have more cachet than they do in most other places. And while it can be readily argued that New Orleans has far more than its fair share of world-class chefs, the roster of celebrity chefs has become ridiculously long.

These days, lists of New Orleans' celebrity chefs usually have at least eight people on them and I've seen rosters that include as many as twenty. In an effort to stabilize the hyperbolized currency, I took out a legal pad and a No. 2 Dixon pencil and tried to come up with a list of local chefs deserving to be considered as bona fide celebrities.

I came up with five and a half names, the half being the

ubiquitous Emeril Lagasse, and the other five being Paul Prudhomme, Susan Spicer, Frank Brigtsen, Donald Link and John Besh.

Lagasse loses his half point because his far flung empire of more than a dozen restaurants across the country, his unrelenting television appearances and his corporate assimilation into the Martha Stewart conglomerate have made him more of a visitor than a resident.

Besh continues to hang on to his full star, despite his growing number of restaurants and increasing television gigs. As of this writing, Besh only has his fingers in seven New Orleans restaurants, the furthest away of which is the charming La Provence across Lake Ponchartrain in Big Branch.

Spicer also flirted with over-expansion several times, but a successful cookbook (*Crescent City Cooking*), happiness in her later-in-life marriage and the continued runaway demand for "New World Cuisine" at her Creole cottage restaurant, Bayona, and the newer Mondo in Lakeview keep her securely harbored in New Orleans.

While Paul Prudhomme, generally credited as the creator and champion of hybrid Louisiana cuisine, turned the day-to-day operation of K-Paul's Louisiana Kitchen over to executive chef Paul Miller, he remains active in recipe development as well as a high profile ambassador for post-Katrina New Orleans and indigenous regional ingredients and cuisine.

Donald Link, a chef with deep bayou country roots, gained attention when he partnered with Susan Spicer in creating Herbsaint, the cozy bistro on the St. Charles streetcar tracks. After taking over the restaurant's day-to-day operations, Link also opened the much discussed Cochon, a combination restaurant and butcher shop specializing in charcuterie.

This brings us to Frank Brigtsen, probably the least known of the celebrity chefs mentioned, due mostly to the fact that he spends the vast majority of his time in the kitchen, doing what a chef should be doing, namely, cooking.

Brigtsen's credentials aren't flashy. A local New Orleans lad, he grew up eating Creole cooking and kicking around city kitchens until he was 24, when he went to work as an apprentice for Paul Prudhomme at Commander's Palace in the middle 1970s. He followed Prudhomme and his late wife when they opened K-Paul's, and served as the initial night chef when the restaurant started serving dinner.

Prudhomme, a Cajun from Opelopusas, is best known for creating blackened redfish and integrating Cajun ingredients into the more urbane Creole cooking then prevalent in New Orleans. This put Brigtsen at the epicenter of the birth of the hydrid Prudhomme referred to as Louisiana Cuisine, and this period of time would have a profound influence on the up and coming chef.

In 1986, with the help of a loan from his mentor Prudhomme, Frank and his wife, Marna, opened Brigtsen's in a shotgun Creole cottage in the Riverbend section of Uptown New Orleans. Located on a quiet side street away from the city's major convention and tourism centers, the restaurant soon became a bustling local "find" and today remains a busy restaurant with a strong in-town following. The restaurant vaulted into the national spotlight when Frank Brigtsen was named "Best Chef, Southeast" in the 1994 James Beard Awards.

Despite its success glittering and national reputation, the restaurant has chosen to remain small in size, the front of the house (literally) confined in three adjoining rooms with an adjacent shotgun hall alongside. The hall is narrow, and tables pack the dining rooms leaving little room for servers to make their ways through the restaurant. With its most gracious staff, one gets the feeling of being at a lively dinner party in a house too small to hold all the guests. This in and of itself is not an unpleasant situation by any means; rather, it gives the restaurant an intimate "clubby" feeling – that of a friendly local place serving inspired food instead of a starchy "temple of cuisine."

While saying that any one restaurant puts out the best plates of food in New Orleans is an invitation to argument, it isn't difficult to make the case that the best food using local ingredients and techniques is coming out of Frank Brigtsen's kitchen. It is "Next Step Louisiana Cuisine," its Cajun and Creole heritages unmistakable, but without the preciousness or over-the-top eccentricities of nouvelle cuisine's outer reaches.

Main courses are straightforward with restrained flourishes. Consider, if you will, a broiled gulf fish with a crabmeat Parmesan crust, mushrooms and a lemon Mousselline sauce. There's a pan-roasted pork tenderloin with sweet potato dirty rice and pork debris or a panéed rabbit with a sesame crust, spinach and Creole mustard sauce. It is cooking with complimentary regional flavors instead of exotic ingredients selected for contrast. It is home cooking as high art.

While Brigtsen changes his menu with the seasons, his seafood platter, by far the restaurant's most frequently ordered entrée, appears year-round. It is a sampler of six items: grilled drum with crawfish and jalapeño lime sauce; shrimp cornbread with jalapeño smoked corn butter; baked oyster LeRuth with shrimp and crabmeat; baked oyster with fennel, jalapeño shrimp cole slaw, and panéed sea scallop with asparagus purée.

The same virtuosity is reflected in the appetizer menu, which regularly offers as many as a dozen choices from such traditional items as a filet gumbo with rabbit and andouille sausage or a shortcake made of crawfish etoufée with a basil black pepper biscuit, to more adventurous offerings such as oysters and artichoke au gratin or sautéed veal sweetbreads with potato leek cake, mushrooms, capers and lemon roasted garlic butter.

Not too long ago, The Sensible One and I were contemplating pushing back from our table and waddling down the narrow corridor when our server sweet-talked us into splitting a piece of Brigtsen's homemade pecan pie, which had been cited on the Food Network TV program *The Best Thing I Ever Ate*, by none less than Southern cuisine author / connoisseur John T. Edge. While I'm not ready to wholeheartedly agree with Mr. Edge's glittering evaluation, it was one superb piece of pie and the empty plate looked terribly sad.

Brigtsen's has now been in business well over twenty years, quite a long time in the restaurant industry, but seemingly the mere blink of an eye in a city where one family has been running a restaurant for 170 years. Yet in these times, when celebrities are ground out of the media machine like so much sausage, there's something refreshing about a man who has quietly built his reputation in his kitchen instead of by chasing press notice and ceaseless self-promotion.

In a quarter century, Brigtsen has done a mere handful of TV appearances compared to many others in the business, and his empire building seems limited to acquiring Charlie's Sea Foods, a family seafood place out on industrial Jefferson Highway. If he keeps doing what he's doing at the level he's doing it, one of these years, Frank Brigtsen is destined to become an overnight success.

Brigtsen's
Louisiana Heritage Cuisine
5.5 miles from The Zero Point
723 Dante Street (next to River Road)
Open 5:30 until 10:00 p.m. for dinner
Tuesday through Saturday
Reservations are strongly encouraged;
all major credit cards are accepted
Telephone: (504) 861-7691
Website: www.brigtsens.com

Mosca's

With Marcello's rising star came rising fortunes, and with them came one Provino Mosca, an Italian emigrant to Chicago who took little time in gathering both a criminal record and an irresistible item on his resumé: personal chef for Al Capone.

AT THE END OF THE OLD WESTERN, *The Man Who Shot Liberty Valance*, a seasoned publisher tells a young buck reporter, "This is the West, sir. When the legend becomes fact, print the legend."

Whenever I hear the line, I think of Mosca's,

If New Orleans is anything, it is a decidedly Southern city. As a lot, Southerners embrace their ghosts, spin yarns about them and if the whole truth happens to get in the way, well, print the legend.

Should you choose to have dinner at Mosca's, and you indeed should, the cab ride from the French Quarter of the CBD (Central Business District) could easily cost more than your meal. You'll get there one of two ways: taking modern highways through the suburban West Bank with its car lots and fast food joints, or by taking a white knuckle roller coaster ride over a rickety Erector set called the Huey Long Bridge, a Depression era span that will likely have you gridlocked in traffic 113 dizzying feet over the Mississippi River, vibrated close to panic by the trains sharing the span, and all the time having a bleak conversation with your own mortality. In fact, my rugged pal "The Marlboro Man" once made the trip with me to Mosca's via the Huey and swore he'd chuck me over the rail if I ever took him across the bridge again.

The first time I was taken to Mosca's, many years ago, I was thoroughly convinced I was about to be killed and eaten. It's in a nondescript, white plank roadhouse on a long, flat stretch of U.S. Highway 90 about five miles west of the rickety bridge. In fact, at first glance, it's easy to mistake the place as abandoned. These days, there are more hints of civilization around it than there used to be, but that's not saying much.

If you arrive after sundown, you'll hear the steady drone of insects and the occasional mating call of frogs from the 178-acre parcel of swamp that runs along the south side of the highway and protects the roadhouse from both sides and the rear. Listen harder and you may start telling yourself you hear the ghosts of several dozen deadbeat gamblers, stool pigeons and double-crossing goombahs, all reputedly wrapped in chains and dispatched to eternity in the slime beneath the marshland's boggy waters.

If anyone knows the whole story about Mosca's, they're not talking, no doubt a wise choice. There's a history section on the restaurant's website, and it tells the story of hardworking, patriotic Italian immigrants who, with grit, gumption, elbow grease and pluck, claimed their modest patch of the American Dream along a forlorn highway. It's a great story, as far as it goes, but the legends surrounding Mosca's suggest it doesn't go far enough.

In its earliest years, the nondescript building was known as the Willswood Tavern, which looked more or less like any roadside bar in any south Louisiana parish. The tavern had once been an abandoned shed on the acreage that was owned by the Marcello family, alleged to have deep Mafia connections. At the end of World War II, Carlos Marcello (1910-1993), known behind his back as "The Little Man," came to be regarded as "boss" of all organized crime operations in New Orleans, and Sundays at the Willswood became legendary.

From Lake Charles in the west to Gulfport (Mississippi) in the east, family captains and lieutenants would make their way to the don's unofficial headquarters at the Willswood to pay tribute (as well as his "taste" of the take) to Marcello. Throughout the morning and into the afternoon, a steady procession of bookies, madams, fences, corrupt law enforcement officials, greased-palm politicos, loan sharks and other "associates" would take care of business with il padrone. Once the serious work was done, rivers of wine would flow, plate upon plate of Italian food would stream out of the kitchen and the raucous party would continue until the shadows grew long and daylight grew short.

With Marcello's rising star came rising fortunes, and with them came one Provino Mosca, an Italian emigrant to Chicago who took little time in gathering both a criminal record and an irresistible item on his resumé: personal chef for Al Capone. Marcello installed Mosca in the kitchen of the Willswood and even went so far as to build a house for the chef's family close to the tavern.

Circa 1960, Marcello moved his headquarters from the

Willswood and the restaurant, already growing famous, became Mosca's. Part of the legend is that the restaurant and the surrounding acreage of swamp were gifted to the Mosca family by Marcello. Maybe that's true and maybe it isn't, but either way, it makes a charming asterisk, so print the legend.

Provino Mosca passed on in 1962, followed by Carlos Marcello in 1993. Over the ensuing years, the restaurant has come to more closely resemble what is written in the website's antiseptic history than the embodiment of a dark and sinister world, which would rightly include black sedans with rolled steel mudguards, the chatter of Thompson submachine guns, whispering godfathers, Mustache Petes, wise guys, goombahs and gun molls. No matter how colorful such imagery may be, the real legend is considerably more flavorful.

More than sixty years after Provino Mosca first walked into the roadhouse kitchen, successive generations of his family continue to put out some of New Orleans' best Sicilian-by-way-of-the-bayou cooking, cucina that earned the restaurant designation as one of "America's Classics" in the 1998 James Beard Awards. In a city where you rarely have to venture more than a few blocks to find superlative food, crowds of local residents continue to risk rickety bridges and desolate miles to pack the place.

The menu is surprisingly short. Only four specialties are listed along with four types of spaghetti, a filet mignon, quail, Cornish hen and a homemade sausage that could very well be the city's gold standard.

The four specialties are worth special note. Least famous among the four is a traditional chicken cacciatore, which allows diners to evaluate the kitchen's comparative chops, considering the ubiquity of the dish in America's Italian restaurants. In the same neighborhood is Chicken à la Grande, the house variation on classic rosemary chicken, but amped up with generous amounts of olive oil, white wine and enough garlic to send Dracula packing back to Transylvania. Somewhat sheepishly, I confess to avoiding the à la Grande on my first visits to Mosca's, mistakenly thinking it would prove a rather pedestrian chicken dish. After one bite, I stood corrected.

The two specialties that attract the most attention are the eponymous Shrimp and Oysters Mosca. Shrimp Mosca is an Italianized adaptation of traditional New Orleans style barbecue shrimp – sautéed in plenty of butter with torqued-up garlic, rosemary and oregano. Despite the similarity in names, the Oysters Mosca are confidently seasoned, topped with a hearty layer of breadcrumbs and baked in an old-fashioned metal pie pan. Both dishes are, in a word, peerless.

Despite the brevity of the menu, it remains a test of indecision. Repeat customers have learned the only practicable formula to remedy their wavering is to bring as many people as they can pack in their car, have everyone order something different, put it all in the center of the table and go after it "family style." The only drawback I've found to this system is that while I get a taste of everything, I never seem to get enough of anything.

Time doesn't have much meaning at Mosca's. Everything is cooked to order, and some dishes take close to an hour to get to the table. This sometimes leads to the staggered delivery of plates, and if all the plates happen to reach your party at the same time, don't be overly surprised if the temperatures prove inconsistent. The only know cure for this situation is another glass of wine. *Cent'anni!*

A couple of caveats are in order. First, they don't take reservations on Saturday night except for very large parties. Even though the restaurant accepts reservations Tuesday through Friday nights, expect a wait, sometimes quite lengthy. Secondly, like many old-line New Orleans restaurants, the only coin of the realm honored is cash.

Finally, in terms of ambience, Mosca's remains an unadorned roadhouse after sixty-plus years, and several generations of New Orleanians wouldn't have it any other way. A nibble here, a nibble there and neither will you.

With all due apologies to the crusty old editor in *The Man Who Shot Liberty Valance*, "Don't print the legend. Eat it."

Mosca's Restaurant
Creole Italian
18.5 miles from The Zero Point
4137 U.S. Highway 90 West, Avondale, Louisiana 70094
Dinner Tuesday through Saturday, 5:30 p.m. to 9:30 p.m.
Only cash is accepted and no reservations
taken on Saturdays, except for large parties
Call 504-436–8950 or 504-436–9942
after 4:30 p.m. to make reservations
Website: www.moscasrestaurant.com

La Provence

*La Provence is a study in understatement and that in itself
is a refreshing departure from the hyper self-consciousness
that seems to swirl around so many restaurants these days.*

DRIVING FORTY MILES to visit a greater New Orleans area
restaurant that owes little of its culinary inspiration, ambience or sense of place to the city itself is perhaps a quirky en-
deavor for a visitor, yet in the case of La Provence, such a
side trip borders on the irresistible.

The place itself feels like it would be more at home on
a French roadside than its setting on a stick-straight stretch
of wooded highway connecting two bedroom communities
containing few features that might separate them from any
other American suburb.

La Provence is now in its second generation, which is a
story in itself. Opened well over a quarter century ago by
chef Chris Keragiorgious, it was taken over upon his death
by a young Marine veteran who had worked as one Keragiorgious' apprentices after returning home from the Gulf
War, and one whose reputation would ultimately eclipse that
of his mentor.

That young executive chef and now owner is John Besh,
a local boy from neighboring Slidell, whose career track
seems to run in eerie parallel with that of Emeril Lagasse.

Besh's first restaurant, August in the Central Business District of New Orleans, skyrocketed to success and was soon followed by a string of new restaurants. A superb cookbook followed, as did a cable network program, and questions have arisen whether Besh's attention will become diluted by being spread across too many projects.

One of the intriguing aspects of Besh's rise in culinary circles, particularly in New Orleans, is that while Lagasse seems to be content replicating his flagship restaurant's success with minimal variations, Besh seems to be committed to nudging the envelope of venue diversity. Consider that at this writing, Besh is running his freestanding flagship restaurant (August), a casino chophouse (Besh Steak), an Alsace-influenced hotel restaurant (Lüke) and its counterpart (also named Lüke) in San Antonio, another hotel restaurant with a rustic Italian motif (Domenica), and a burger/meatloaf/comfort food outlet in the National World War II Museum (The American Sector) as well as La Provence. On top of this, he has just announced partnership in yet another restaurant named "Borgone," which will feature dishes with culinary roots in the Canary Islands.

Besh has long been a staunch advocate of combining native Louisiana foodstuffs with French-inspired techniques to produce a localized bistro cuisine, probably a holdover from his days as an apprentice for Keragiorgious, who along with Pierre Lacoste were among the earliest champions of the culinary hybrid. Today, of course, it seems that almost every restaurant that covers its tables in white broadcloth describes itself as "Old World cuisine with Local Flair." But to Besh's everlasting credit, he carries the notion far past le cliché nouveau and puts it into committed practice, particularly at La Provence.

Ever since its earliest days as Keragiorgious' back-country atelier, a central feature of La Provence has been its herb garden, which guarantees not only freshness but also local authenticity. After taking the reins at La Provence, Besh installed his own Berkshire hog farm, where the hogs are bred and fed organic scraps from the kitchens of his restaurants, before being slaughtered and processed in Besh's on-premises smokehouse. Every part of the hog is used somewhere in Besh's growing empire, from feet being slow-cooked to create the pieds de conchon at Lüke, skin for cracklings used at August to the livers being used in the ramekins of pâté that grace every table inside neighboring La Provence.

Such devotion to centuries-old cooking techniques and hair-splitting attention to detail are no doubt contributors to Besh's increasing cachet in national culinary circles, but when viewing La Provence as a whole instead of a corporate component, I find something re-assuring in the fact that such persnickety steps are never mentioned. One of the pure joys of La Provence, at least for The Sensible One and me, is its lack of fussiness or Gallic posturing. The wait staff doesn't ooze blatantly fake chumminess and the everyday chef de cuisine remains anonymous instead of being the reigning centerpiece in a cult of personality. La Provence is a study in understatement and that in itself is a refreshing departure from the hyper self-consciousness that seems to swirl around so many restaurants these days.

When I first pull into the restaurant's parking lot, my

internal clock readjusts itself to a gentler pace and in the seconds it takes to walk through the trellised archway and the small front door, my frame of mind has become that of an unhurried sightseer on holiday in a sunlit corner of France. There is a cozy waiting room inside with comfortable furniture and French magazines to thumb though, a pleasant enough place for a short wait and perhaps an aperitif to stimulate the appetite before being led to your table.

There are a couple of small dining rooms on either side of a crackling, whitewashed fireplace in the main restaurant. The ceilings are low and the yellow ochre walls remain mostly unadorned. Arched openings along the walls afford you with a view of a large barroom with another fireplace, a grand piano and little furniture on the Oriental rugs, leading me to believe the room sees more use for wedding receptions and private parties. French doors open onto a patio and fountain. Overall, the room has the air of a large villa that has been transformed into a small inn.

Though the main business at La Provence is dinner served Wednesday through Sunday evenings, The Sensible One and I are partial to Sunday brunch, particularly on drab, drizzly days that can only be warmed by a fireplace, robust fare and a bottle of steadfast Burgundy. In fact, on numerous trips over the past decade, we have planned our New Orleans arrival to follow on the heels of a dawdling brunch Provençal.

The food is unfussy French in the finest sense of both words. On a recent visit, The Sensible One started with a roasted chestnut ravioli finished with brown butter, sage and crispy ham, followed by jumbo Louisiana shrimp and butternut squash risotto with Meyer lemon and sage. Her decision was quick compared to mine, as I agonized over choices including Bouillabaisse, swordfish picatta, blue crab bisque, quail gumbo and a "pissaladière" (a warm pizza of onions, anchovies and olives). I finally decided to keep with close to home roots by ordering the Creole turtle soup, followed by a traditional Louisiana slow-cooked cochon du lait, which included braised shoulder, crisp belly and seared tenderloin served with haricorts verts and oven-roasted tomatoes. There's no reason to try and string superlatives; it was all, in a word, superb, as was the apple tart we shared for dessert.

Were it only for the dissimilarities in the restaurants he creates, Besh would be a chef/entrepreneur worth keeping an eye on, but he brings a lot more to the party. Still in his mid-forties and blessed with frat boy good looks, a shaggy mop of hair and an engaging enthusiasm, Besh is a natural for television. Indeed, several years ago he finished a hair's-breadth second to Michael Symon on the Food Network's *Next Iron Chef* series, and in 2010 launched a series of his own, *Inedible to Incredible,* on The Learning Channel. Seeming to have enough energy to make the Energizer Bunny look like a slacker, Besh has still another program on public television, *My New Orleans*, based upon a handsome cookbook of the same name. Far more telegenic and less inclined to hijack center stage at the expense of his guests than Emeril Lagasse, whose early career Besh seems to almost channel, many industry insiders seem to believe that the future is as much in front of Besh as it is behind Lagasse.

If Besh continues to grow into a national personality to

the point his commitments put more pressure on his time and attention than his New Orleans activities require, it will be a great loss to one of America's premier cities' culinary landscapes.

To realize how much of a loss that would be, one only has to drive forty miles from downtown New Orleans to savor the near miracles that occur when home-grown ingredients meet a reverence for time-honored cooking principles under the watchful eyes of John Besh. One need go no further than La Provence.

La Provence
Louisiana French
41.0 miles from The Zero Point
25020 Highway 190
Big Branch, Louisiana 70445
Dinner served Wednesday through Sunday evenings
Bruch served Sunday
Reservations are recommended
and credit cards are honored
Telephone: (985) 626-7662
Website: www.laprovencerestaurant.com

II.
LOCAL FLAVOR

Central to any New Orleans dining experience is discovering food that was born in the city herself. While such fare can be found in far more places than the following essays, the restaurants contained herein offer not only local cooking or creations, they also provide settings where, in most cases, the diners are predominantly local.

The possible glaring exception to this is Central Grocery on Decatur Street across from the French Market, one of the most visited sites in the city. Yet it was in this Italian groceria where one of the city's most iconic foods, the muffuletta, was created early in the last century.

While Pascal's Manale and the original Drago's on suburban Arnoult Street can certainly be construed as "nice" restaurants if not terribly fancy, the remaining three are true neighborhood joints where the portions are generous, the chow is terrific and the accents are both local and thick. They're not easy to find, require cab rides for visitors without vehicles, are equally unassuming and all offer a rewarding experience, both culinary and cultural, for the adventurous diner in search of neighborhood "cuisine."

Central Grocery Co.

The most practical solution is to grab as many paper napkins as you can get away with, wear old clothes and dig in.

THE OLD NEIGHBORHOOD is mostly gone now. There's not much that's French about the historic French Market and, for that matter, there's not all that much market about it, either.

For more than half a century, the area was New Orleans' "Little Italy," but subsequent generations of immigrant Italian families emigrated first to Mid-City, then the suburbs, leaving the lower Decatur Street area without much of a cohesive identity.

You'll still find a few trattorias and pizza joints tucked between Mardi Gras bead shops, Goth bars, boutiques prone to turnover, glorified convenience stores pumping ear-splitting zydeco into the streets and what appears to be a post-hippie, seemingly lost generation of runaways looking for something – meaning perhaps. You'll find just about as much authentic Italiana at Olive Garden.

Yet in the middle of all this scrambled identity is an unassuming storefront. The address is 923 Decatur Street, and the name of the place couldn't be more generic – Central Grocery Company – but take one step inside and you're an ocean away in Palermo.

In the commercialized, Americanized lower half of the French Quarter, Central Grocery is the last paisano standing. Established in 1906, the storefront groceria has outlived countless competitors to gain a special standing in the hearts of New Orleanians.

While it may be true that time has taken its toll on Central Grocery, which keeps chipping away snippets of its charm more for the convenience of the people who work there and less for those who shop and buy, you only need to have one foot in the door and you immediately know you've stepped into the Old World, redolent with garlic, cheese, olive oil, salami and so many other heady scents of home cooking, Siciliana style.

The front half of the room, which is the actual grocery store, is a treasure trove for aficionadi della cucina italiana, especially those who revel in its preparation. As generations passed, shelf space became so premium that the store's inventory began expanding vertically instead of horizontally, forcing customers to carefully squeeze their way through tight aisles between tall shelves and display cases of imported Italian foodstuffs. In addition to tins and jars of peppers, olives, squid, anchovies, biscotti and more, you'll find boxes of imported pasta, cases of salamis and cheese, loose beans and lentils sold from the barrel and even the stray dried stockfish from time to time.

At its core, Central may be an old fashioned groceria, but the true heartbeat of the place is the muffuletta, the city's signature Italian sandwich, the creation of which is generally accredited to the store.

The muffuletta is named for its bread, a crusty round loaf eight or nine inches in diameter. The loaf is stuffed with Cappicola ham, Genoa salami, mortadella and provolone, but what gives the enormous sandwich its true character is the olive salad that's piled upon the meat and cheese. It is sold and served in quarters, and a workable rule of thumb is that two of those quarters will usually satisfy anyone this side of a famished longshoreman.

Olive salad hearkens back to the days when olives were shipped in wooden barrels of brine. In transit, and even in the groceria, the weight of the olives in the top of the barrel would crush a number of those at the bottom, rendering them undesirable to the consumers of the day, who were willing to pay full olive price only for full olives. Enterprising grocers would add garlic cloves, capers, parsley and oregano to the broken olives, chop up produce that had gone unsold, and then mix it all in olive oil and red wine vinegar. The result was not only a savory condiment, but also a highly efficient way to make use of inventory otherwise going to waste.

Although olive salad is its most common name, people with a bent for linguistics may find it interesting to know that for the better part of the Twentieth Century, the concoction was generally referred to as "wop salad." While modern cultural sensitivity and political correctness have more or less relegated the term to the lexicological scrap heap, it still appears on some old-line New Orleans menus (most notably at Rocky & Carlo's, a workingman's Italian restaurant in the blue-collar suburb of Chalmette).

To accommodate rushes of business at noontime and

the end of the day, the staff at Central Grocery fabricates muffulettas throughout the day. Surprisingly, to a great many people, the longer the sandwich sits unsold, the better it becomes because the olive oil in the salad soaks into the bread itself. Yes, it is messy, but eating a quarter of a muffuletta without having something spill out of the sandwich is an art few people have ever mastered. The most practical solution is to grab as many paper napkins as you can get away with, wear old clothes and dig in.

The back half of Central Grocery provides some very limited areas for eating in, but it is a cramped and soulless place, an obvious afterthought that commandeered valuable and profitable merchandise shelf space.

Far more pleasant it is to pick up a muffuletta and a Barq's root beer, walk a block to the levee and enjoy an impromptu picnic on a bench, watching the ships glide by and feeling the breezes of the Great American River. Or walk two blocks up Decatur Street, grab one of the benches in the circle surrounding the statue of "Old Hickory" in Jackson Square, and listen for the bells of the city's iconic St. Louis Cathedral.

One thing you might want to keep in mind before you enter Central Grocery for the first time is that the people who work there are an inexplicably surly bunch of characters, who take all aspects of play out of playful gruffness as if intent on elevating rudeness to an art form. In fact, it's easier to find more convivial Italian gents on the losing side of a soccer match, driving taxis in Rome or brandishing cabbages when the tenor hits a clinker. Why this may be so eludes me, but I find the best way to get around this is, when they treat me as if I'm nothing but another handful of cash, to ignore them right back.

Before you ask, yes, Central Grocery has muffulettas tightly wrapped in plastic and butcher paper and ready to go back to the airport with you. It is hardly uncommon to be standing somewhere in a Louis Armstrong New Orleans International concourse and catch a whiff of garlicky olive salad in someone's purse or carry-on as it passes by. (I can't help but wonder what the life expectancy is of a fragrant muffuletta in a jam-packed airplane that's sitting on the tarmac waiting in line to take off or, even worse, for one of those mysterious delays that last an eternity or two.)

Along those same lines, quart jars of olive salad are available for those who don't want the temptation of a whole sandwich under their nose. Perhaps it's just me, but for years, I used to carry them home only to discover the seal was loose enough that oil seeped out onto the label and down the side of the jar, so you might want to make sure the seal is good and tight before you leave the store.

Like most dishes created by New Orleans eateries, the muffuletta has fostered a multitude of imitators not only in the city, but regionally. Many feature a slight variation on ingredients; Napoleon House serves theirs warm, Liuzza's on Bienville Street serves a "Frenchuletta" on French bread instead of the traditional Italian loaf, and a few years ago even Emeril Lagasse developed his own muffuletta pizza recipe. As happens in such cases, some of these have attracted their own followings, but those seeking the real deal need only sample l'originale at Central.

And feel free to snarl right back at the surly *pagliacco* behind the counter.

Central Grocery Company
Muffulettas
0.3 miles from The Zero Point
923 Decatur Street
(between Dumaine and St. Philip Streets)
Open Tuesday – Saturday, 9:00 a.m. – 5:00 p.m.
Major credit cards accepted
Telephone: (504) 523-1620
No website

Pascal's Manale

Considering that the provenance of New Orleans Barbecue Shrimp was a comedy of errors, it should come as no surprise that no one could agree upon the best way to cook it, either.

THE NAME IS MISLEADING, the history appears to keep revising itself, no one seems to agree on how the dish is prepared and the most commonly asked question is, "What's a Manale, anyway?"

Generally regarded as one of the most iconic dishes in the entire New Orleans Creole-Italian repertoire, Barbecue Shrimp has absolutely nothing to do with barbecue in the way you probably know it. There's no hickory or mesquite, the sauce isn't tomato based and sweetened with either brown sugar or molasses, and people in Kansas City and Memphis (and Texas and the Carolinas) don't argue about whose is best.

This much is known, or at least widely accepted, or maybe suspected: New Orleans Barbecue Shrimp came into being sometime during the mid-1950s in the kitchen of an Italian family restaurant named Pascal's Manale. Opened in 1913 by one Frank Manale, the Napoleon Avenue restaurant eventually found its way into the hands of Manale's nephew, Pascal Radosta, who decided to rename the place after both of them.

Legend has it that on that fateful evening in the 1950s, one of the regular customers named Vincent Sutro had just returned from a business trip to Chicago and started singing the praises of a dish he'd eaten there that, as far as he could remember, had shrimp, butter and a lot of pepper in it. He asked Pascal's chef, Jake Radosta, if he could make some, and the chef said he could try.

Chef Radosta went into the kitchen, cooked up something that was as close as he could get to the fellow's vague description and waited while the man tasted it. After a taste or two, the man said it wasn't what he'd eaten in Chicago. It was better.

Owner Radosta decided to put it on the menu, where it's stayed ever since. No one knows where the name came from. One guess was that this all happened at the point in time when the suburban backyard barbecuing craze was at its zenith and, despite being a misnomer, the name was coined to cash in on the fad. Whether that's true or not, there is a delicious irony about a misrepresented recipe being given a misleading name and still becoming a New Orleans classic.

Considering that the provenance of New Orleans Barbecue Shrimp was a comedy of errors, it should come as no surprise that no one could agree upon the best way to cook it, either.

There are two leading schools of thought on the dish's preparation and the advocates of each are pompously cocksure that they are correct. The first is that all the ingredients are mixed in a baking dish and put in the oven, and it would not surprise me to learn that this is how the dish was originally prepared in the kitchen at Pascal's Manale. The alternative belief is that the whole process is accomplished on the stovetop in a cast iron skillet.

I have a sneaking hunch both factions are correct, based upon an item I read several years ago that claimed the dish's widespread popularity actually occurred when it was re-worked by Paul Prudhomme at his newly opened K-Paul's Louisiana Kitchen. Prudhomme is a notoriously fast chef well known for cooking with blazing heat at high speeds, and it seems logical that the creator of blackened redfish would rethink a time-honored recipe for ease and speed of preparation in a commercial kitchen.

In writing this, I wanted to be as accurate as possible, so I went to the Internet to do a comprehensive recipe search. There are dozens of them, including numerous ones claiming to be the original recipe, and these "authentic" guidelines cite both cooking techniques. Well, of course they do. All things considered, it wouldn't be real barbecue shrimp if people could actually agree on its preparation.

But no matter which method of preparation is used, the results are so similar that it takes a true culinary maestro to tell which method was employed. The four driving, traditional flavors are fresh Louisiana shrimp, an exceedingly generous amount of pepper, garlic and enough butter to make a cardiologist scream uncle. Varying recipes call for shrimp stock, Worcestershire, Italian herbs, mint sprigs, Tabasco, white wine, cream and even tomatoes. It is a remarkably flexible dish that readily accommodates any number of personal touches.

There is some disagreement (of course there is) of

whether the Louisiana shrimp should be cooked beheaded, peeled and deveined or intact so the fat contained in the shrimp heads can be incorporated into the sauce.

Essential to any preparation is an abundance of crusty French bread to sop up the peppery butter sauce.

When you order barbecue shrimp at Pascal's Manale, a bib is de rigueur. Peeling the shrimp is part of the process, and before the empty plate is taken away, your fingers will be butter-soaked, and possibly wet from licking them (providing no one is looking). Of course you'll look silly; every adult in a bib looks silly, so get over it. One of the latter meals my late father and I had together was at Pascal's Manale, and all these years later, I treasure the memory of our laughing and pointing at each other in our stupid bibs.

Despite the restaurant's age and success, it still retains the aura of a neighborhood, family place. Located on a corner in a shaded, residential area, Pascal's is set in an unobtrusive building on Dryades Street, which also features an old-line steak house named Charlie's, and an unusual structure originally built by the Mexican consulate that now is home to the city's most discreet bed-and-breakfast, complete with a clothing-optional swimming pool.

From the street, you enter a large, wood-paneled waiting room that also houses the restaurant's cocktail area and oyster bar. It's a friendly, lively area, which is good because some people spend a considerable amount of time there. Like many New Orleans neighborhood places, Pascal's has an unwritten policy of moving guests, even those with reservations, down the line when an old friend or regular decides to drop in – and with nearly a century under its belt, the restaurant has an impressive number of friends. While the waits are usually not inordinately long, a little patience is recommended, as are a cocktail and a dozen of the city's better oysters.

There are two medium-sized dining rooms in the place, the motif of one leaning toward sports, and the other seemingly planned to be a "nice" family place, but somehow it ended up looking like the parlor in a cathouse.

Beyond the barbecue shrimp, the menu doesn't stray far from the predictable -- some veal dishes, a couple of steaks, seafood grilled or fried. While the shrimp is certainly the headliner at Pascal's, the other dishes are treated like anything other than afterthoughts. It's a good kitchen, the kind anyone has the right to expect of a place that's had nearly a century to work out the kinks.

While the dinnertime mood at Pascal's is jovial, the bibs ludicrous, and the food quality normally hovering somewhere between very good and excellent, lunch at the restaurant offers one of the city's exceptional bargains. A small loaf of French bread is hollowed out, filled with barbecue shrimp swimming in its peppery butter and served as a sandwich. While bibs are recommended, I've managed the sandwiches with a number of napkins and minimal wardrobe damage.

Summarizing Pascal's Manale is a challenge, at least for me. The food is very, very good, but I can tick off a dozen places that offer better cooking without breaking a sweat. There's a reason for that, and it afflicts several of the city's more legendary kitchens. For more than fifty years, Pascal's has been able to claim itself as the originator of New Orleans barbecue shrimp, but with that title comes a tacit obligation not to vary one iota from the recipe as originally developed. In the meantime, innovative chefs have enjoyed an open field in which to tinker with and tweak the dish, and this has doubtlessly led to some improvements on the original.

Such a fate is not new; it has befallen such venerable culinary institutions as Oysters Rockefeller and soufflé potatoes at Antoine's, the muffuletta as created by Central Grocery Company, the charbroiled oysters developed at Drago's and many others. It begs the question, at what point does a dish as originally developed become a museum piece, a culinary curiosity overshadowed by the creation of a chef enjoying the freedom to explore and innovate? The truth is, there's often a very real difference between a dish that's been invented and one that's been perfected, but they are both of interest to the dedicated "foodie."

For whichever reason you'd consider a visit to Pascal's Manale, historical or hedonistic, chances are you won't be disappointed.

Pascal's Manale
Creole Italian
3.3 miles from The Zero Point
1838 Napoleon Avenue (at Dryades St.)
Lunch served Monday - Friday, 11:30 a.m. – 2:00 p.m.
Dinner served Monday through Saturday,
5:00 p.m. until closing
Dark Sunday
All major credit cards accepted
Reservations strongly recommended
but not accepted for 5 or more at 7:30 or 8 p.m.
Telephone: (504) 895-4877
Website: www.neworleansrestaurants.com/pascalsmanale

Drago's

How many shuckers must it take to pop open
nearly eleven thousand oysters in a day?
How much butter does it take? Parmesan? Garlic?

DRAGO'S HAS A LONG MENU, in fact one that's ridiculously long considering that most of the people who come in appear to be ordering one item.

That item is Charbroiled Oysters, a house creation that's become the most widely imitated New Orleans dish since Paul Prudhomme blackened his first redfish and launched a national craze.

The Drago's concept is remarkably simple, so much so that the only thing really remarkable is that no one thought of it until 1993, when second generation manager Tommy Cvitanovich poured some house barbecue drumfish sauce (butter, garlic and a handful of herbs) over some oysters on the half shell, sprinkled a little parmesan cheese on top and slapped it on the charcoal grill. The finished oysters are served in a generous amount of the sauce with enough ficelles to sop it up.

These days, according to the company website, the restaurant's two locations put out about 900 dozen charbroiled oysters on a busy day. Stop and think, and the math becomes staggering. How many shuckers must it take to pop open nearly eleven thousand oysters in a day? How much butter does it take? Parmesan? Garlic? On the sales side of the equation, how many family-owned restaurants with only two locales gross several million a year? On one item?

In light of the restaurant's runaway success since 1993, it's difficult to put the previous twenty-four years of Drago's operations in proper context. When Drago and Klara Cvitanovich first opened for business in 1969, they were just another mom-and-pop team trying to carve out a niche in the Metairie family restaurant marketplace, although their Croatian heritage gave them an inside track.

Since settling in Louisiana and along the Mississippi Gulf Coast in the middle of the Nineteenth Century, Croatian-Americans have been the backbone of the region's oystering business. From seeding to harvesting, shucking and serving, successive generations of Croatians have been a mainstay of the industry, and it has long been believed, whether warranted or not, that the most preferred oysters have been held in reserve for "family" eateries.

Success for Croatians in the New Orleans restaurant industry has become a tradition. Until the restaurant's sale in 2011, the Vodanovich family operated Bozo's (a Croation nickname for "Christopher) since the venerable seafood house opened in 1928. Uglesich's opened in 1924 as a sandwich shop, but by the time it closed in May of 2005, three months before Hurricane Katrina, the ten-table restaurant in an iffy part of Central City had developed a national reputation for innovative seafood recipes. The Vojkovich family opened Crescent City Steakhouse in the city's Seventh Ward in 1934, and with the exception of a few JazzFest posters on the wall, the city's oldest family-operated steakhouse looks very much the same as it did on opening night.

Located on a sleepy side street not far from New Orleans' largest shopping center, Drago's steadily built an enviable family business trade. Despite numerous expansions to the building and seemingly endless redecoration, what is now a major enterprise with more than three hundred employees manages to retain the family attitude and ambience that stretches back over forty years to the restaurant's beginning. This is reflected in the menu's comparative length and in the demeanor of the wait staff, some of whom look experienced enough to have their service stretch back to Day One.

The foundation of the lengthy menu, not surprisingly is local seafood, cooked in any number of ways. These are augmented by prime rib, veal, chicken, pasta dishes and one incongruous item called "Shuckee Duckee," a blackened duck breast served over linguini and finished with oysters in a cream sauce. The entrees, and there are eighteen of them listed as specials, tend to run toward the complex in their preparation, the simplest being the traditional prime rib plate and the most complex appearing to be the Barbecue Drumfish (according to the menu a "Drumfish filet, lightly seasoned with fresh herbs, butter, and garlic grilled over an open flame. Served with fresh crabmeat and shrimp dressing, then topped with a crabmeat cream sauce").

Despite such a panoply of entrees, Drago's makes a point of emphasizing its live Maine lobsters. The live boilers start at a pound and go to well over three (listed as "Super Stud" on the menu), and the house also serves them stuffed or sauced three different ways. From my point of view as a visitor, there is something slightly anomalous about being in one of the world's legendary seafood cities and ordering lobster from the frigid waters north of Boston, but I suppose even the denizens of paradise hanker for change from time to time.

In the name of full disclosure, I must tell you that I know very little about the food beyond the Charbroiled Oysters except what I read on the menu and observe when the occasional plate of something besides the oysters passes by on its way to another table.

What's the point?

When we visit Drago's, The Sensible One and I always start with a dozen each of charbroiled oysters before ordering another half dozen or more. Our record is five dozen, and the thing that makes me happiest is that the number of oysters presented is always divisible by two, which prevents an eye-to-eye showdown over the final bivalve and undoubtedly less than chivalrous behavior on my part.

In recent years, Drago's has opened a second operation in the Hilton Riverside at the foot of Poydras Street. The food may be the same, but the place isn't. In fact, compared to the original location, it's remarkably sterile. While the original retains the feel of a flourishing family business, the Hilton location retains the feel of, well, a Hilton.

For some visitors, food is food, a slightly interesting single step above fuel, and ambience is a minor concern. To the true experience seeker, the physical surroundings and service are as integral parts of a restaurant's total flavor as the food. The Hilton's downtown location, a couple of blocks from the French Quarter, is certainly more convenient for most visitors to the city. Whether or not ambient authenticity is important to you as a visitor is truly a matter of choice; either way, the oysters are great.

The runaway success of Drago's charbroiled oysters has led, of course, to any number of restaurants imitating the dish, as happens with any new and successful recipe. In some cases, a dish is invented by one chef, but perfected by another. The Sensible One and I have a tendency to want to try a dish in its original configuration, which sends us searching for its point of origin. Perhaps we're missing something newer and improved, but in the case of charbroiled oysters, we find ourselves returning time and again to the source – because improving on perfection is a mighty tall order.

Drago's Seafood Restaurant
Charbroileld Oysters
Original Location:
8.5 miles from The Zero Point
3232 N. Arnoult Rd, Metairie
Open Mondays - Saturdays, 11:00 a.m. – 9:00 p.m.
Closed Sundays
Closed All Major Holidays, July 4 - July 6,
Mardi Gras weekend and some parade nights
Telephone: (504) 888-9254

In the Hilton New Orleans Riverside:
0.5 miles from The Zero Point
2 Poydras Street
Open Mondays - Saturdays, 11:00 a.m. until 10:00 p.m.
Closed Sundays
Holiday schedule varies
Telephone: (504) 584-3911
Both restaurants accept all major credit cards
No reservations
Website: www.dragosrestaurant.com

R&O's

*Perhaps the best way to describe the extensive menu
is "Round up the usual suspects."*

I'M NOT ONE who cheerfuly stand in ine. Waiting in line for a table doesn't raise my expectations, only my blood pressure. Even at my favorite New Orleans restaurant, Galatoire's, when I see the line extend more than twenty-five feet from the front door, I vamoose.

Consequently, the first time I entered the wraparound entryway of R&O's in the Bucktown neighborhood, the sight of fifteen benches and a dozen stray chairs ready to accommodate fifty-some customers far more patient than me made for an ominous start. Fortunately, with her unfathomable forbearance of my hair-trigger curmudgeonliness, The Sensible One gently pointed out that the restaurant had just opened for the day and there remained a few tables as empty as the foyer benches.

Truth told, any waiting area one-third the size of the restaurant within often means one of three things:

1. The proprietor is a cockeyed optimist.

2. The owner is hoping that the large waiting area will give the impression of a huge demand for seating and thereby generate a snowball effect.

3. The place is really that good.

R&O's is that good.

Trying to put a finger on my basis for such a conclusion, I can't come up with one single reason. Rather, I think R&O's is one of those cases where, to trot out that dreadful cliché, the whole is greater than the sum of its parts.

Despite only dating back to 1980, R&O's is a latter-day continuation of the New Orleans tradition of opening as another kind of business before becoming a restaurant. Parkway, one of the city's premier poor boy shops, began life as a Mid-City bakery. Mandina's, considered by many the city's definitive neighborhood restaurant, started selling sandwiches when it was a pool hall. The legendary Mosca's evolved from a swamp-side roadhouse named Wildwood Tavern. R&O's, the subject at hand, started in the tiny back room of a ramshackle grocery store.

A true Mom & Pop operation, R&O's (so dubbed for founders Roland and Ora) expanded into first a pizza parlor before expanding once again into its current incarnation of poor boy, platter and pizza emporium. While many if not most restaurants seem to lose momentum in proportion to expansion, that isn't the case at R&O's, which seems to have expanded its customer base even more rapidly than its real estate.

For the type of place it is, R&O's is relatively large with a capacity in the neighborhood of 150 people. When the restaurant is full, and it often is, the members of the wait staff have to carefully maneuver trays between the tables, improvising and then to navigating impossibly narrow walkways. The attendant noise level puts R&O high on the list of restaurants you'd be least likely to select for a romantic meal, but that's not the point of the place anyway.

Ultimately, R&O's is not a place to "dine" in the most elegant sense of the word. Rather, it seems to be the first place anyone on the west suburban part of the city thinks of when someone says, "Let's go get something to eat."

The room is as Saturday afternoon casual as the dress code. Multicolored Christmas tree lights line the inside rafters. No matter where you sit, you'll be sure to see a poster, banner, newspaper front page, brewery sign or knick-knack celebrating the city's beloved NFL Saints. Despite food that can sometimes prove messy to eat, there are no napkins provided or napkin holders on the tables, but instead rolls of paper towels on vertical stands serve that utilitarian purpose.

As one might expect in a place that clearly caters to a local, middle class clientele, the servers, mostly middle-aged women, somehow manage to keep smiles on their faces while ceaselessly hustling an army's worth of food through tight spaces to ravenous hordes. Despite the fact that I find myself older than the majority of them, the way they coddle and cluck over me whisks me back a half-century to suppertime at Mom's kitchen table.

The drawing card at R&O's is the food, period, and there is nothing fancy, pretentious or precious about it. It is straightforward New Orleans casual with a Sicilian "red gravy" accent. Perhaps the best way to describe the extensive menu is "Round up the usual suspects." Consider:

• The menu lists eighteen appetizers ranging from seasonal boiled shellfish to French fries smothered in gravy

• There are three soups and a half dozen salads

• Twenty-five sandwiches are listed before add-ons, from the ubiquitous muffuletta to soft-shell crab Parmesan served on sesame-seeded Italian rolls instead of the more traditional poor boy loaf

• Eight mostly Italian specials are offered at weekday lunch

• Thin or thick crust pizzas, both hand-tossed, are available with a choice of twenty toppings

• The twenty-four dinner choices are mainly seafood, Sicilian or a traditional hybrid of the two

• A true, kid-friendly family place, R&O's offers nine children's plates of real food (with not a hot dog, hamburger or chicken tender in sight).

Even by New Orleans standards, the portions are generous. Plus, for the underfed itinerant lumberjack or the garden-variety masochist, there are three desserts on the menu and usually a couple of chalkboard suggestions.

The cooking is not imaginative, but workmanlike, and that may be the true secret of R&O's continuing success.

Even in New Orleans, a city where kitchens seem to be abandoning homegrown traditional cuisine in favor of the trickiest post-hip trend and so-called (and often self-styled) celebrity / superstar chefs sprouting up like so much culinary crabgrass, the number of people deriving comfort from the familiar far exceeds the vocal minority of fad chasers. While I do not have the statistics at hand, I would be willing to wager that during R&O's 32-year run of dishing up dependability, it's far more likely that the number of gimmick-chasing eateries that have opened and shuttered their doors can be more easily counted by the hundred than the dozen.

In all candor, were I able to have time for only one meal on a trip to New Orleans, it would more likely be at a place that's more upscale than R&O's. There are, after all, any number of restaurants in New Orleans where the cooking is more heroic, the servers more polished and the surroundings more genteel.

That said, there remains a school of thought suggesting that if you want to learn what the city it truly all about, the farther you get away from the established tourism and convention districts, the closer to its heart you'll get.

You may very well take exception to such a statement, and that's more than okay, but I know of a place where more than fifty people with growling stomachs patiently sit on wooden benches waiting to disagree.

R&O's
Poor boys, Platters & Pizza
8.4 miles from The Zero Point
216 Old Hammond Highway in Metairie
Open for lunch daily,
for dinner Wednesday through Sunday
All major credit cards honored
No reservations
Telephone (501) 831-1248
No website

Brocato's Eat Dat

*For the most part, it's Cajun plate lunch fare
and it's damn good.*

IT SEEMS THAT WHENEVER a shoestring restaurateus is knocked for lack of décor or ambience, the inevitable response is a growled, "You don't eat da atmosphere, buddy."

Well, maybe not, but no one in their right mind would ever deny that the vibe of the room itself is a vital component of any total, holistic restaurant event. Imagine, if you will, a bag burger in a room filled with sparkling chandeliers, or perhaps a terrine of pâté de fois gras being dished up in a hash house.

Over the years, such stunts have been attempted any number of times across America by "creative" restaurateurs with predictable results. Such juxtaposition of cuisine and ambience is more often an exercise in self-conscious eccentricity than genuine creativity and most diners see the prank for what it is, a one-time joke. Yawn.

Now and then, however, someone comes along and makes such a juxtaposition work, even though in the case of Brocato's Eat Dat in East New Orleans, I suspect such a serendipitous result is more a case of under-capitalization than intent.

Had I not heard some buzz about good food coming

out of the Eat Dat kitchen, I would have never driven the eleven miles or so to look for the place. After all, East New Orleans and St. Bernard Parish are hardly hotbeds of the city's great restaurants, and beyond Rocky & Carlo's in Chalmette, most locals would be hard-pressed to name a restaurant in the area. Hell, most of then probably couldn't even name Rocky & Carlo's despite the fact the macaroni and cheese there is the stuff of local epicurean legend.

Consider the restaurant's ambience or perhaps the lack thereof. To get to Eat Dat, you drive alongside a drainage canal in a middle- to lower-middle class neighborhood until you reach what appears to be a most unsuccessful, white cement block strip center. There's a photographer's studio at the back of the center, some space available at the front, and somewhere near the middle are two generic doors under a vinyl banner. A discount store neon OPEN sign flickers behind one of the door windows.

You enter a relatively large dining hall, large enough that the institutional tables and chairs are widely spread out to fill two-thirds of the high-ceilinged room. Next to the front door is a whiteboard where the day's specials are scrawled, and it's the first time you even get an inkling that the place might be far better than it looks. A second inkling comes when you look around only to discover that the place is crawling with more cops than a raid at a topless club. While The Sensible One and I were having lunch one day, nine – count 'em, nine – of New Orleans' finest came through for either sit-down or carry-out lunches. The city's boys and girls in blue may not know how to do a lot about crime, but they do know how to eat and walking in on a bevy of them is a definite harbinger of good eats to come.

While some restaurateurs would never spare a single dime decorating their dining rooms, I'm not altogether sure that Eat Dat owner/chef Troy Brocato even forked over the first nickel. The walls are covered with whitish wallpaper that was probably part of the landlord's low cost build-out. A cluster of fleur de lis bric-a-brac hangs higgledy-piggledy on one of the walls. Were it suggested that the room has any visual center at all, it would come from a blown-up sticker of a Saints helmet not unlike those found in the bedrooms of pre-adolescent schoolboys. The floor is covered with a gray, industrial grade carpeting that seems better suited to a window-peeping private eye's office, and the whole room features a noticeably high drop ceiling studded with fluorescent lights. Taken as a whole, the dining room looks not so much like a restaurant as it does the suicide note of a hopelessly inept decorator.

Despite the fact that such harsh lighting and uninspired décor provide a natural showcase for the unavoidable spills, drops, oops and other calamities of an intrinsically messy industry, the dining room at Brocato's Eat Dat is boot camp spotless. Such cleanliness, I think, is not merely the predictable residue of diligence, but rather testament to a ferocious pride that starts with Troy Brocato and runs all the way through his small staff to the guy who bags the garbage and schleps it to the dumpster.

Brocato's Eat Dat is on its surface a nondescript neighborhood place in a nondescript neighborhood, but at its very heart exists an unexpected confluence of heritage and birthright that manifests itself on steaming platters of classic Louisiana cuisine, the recipes for many of which start with the simple words, "First, make a roux."

New Orleanians not in the know make the honest and understandable mistake of assuming that Brocato is a scion of the Sicilian family of confectioners whose gelati, cannoli and biscotti have been revered in the city for over a century. In truth, owner/chef Troy Brocato is an Opelousas lad, part of another family that has become synonymous with Cajun heritage cooking and its fusion into the Louisiana culinary mainstream – the Prudhommes. In point of fact, Troy Brocato's great-uncle is the legendary Paul Prudhomme, creator of blackened redfish in his celebrated K-Paul's restaurant and generally regarded as the godfather of updated Louisiana cuisine.

Brocato worked for thirteen years in his great-uncle's Chartres Street kitchen, where chef Prudhomme, and later Paul Miller, always emphasized both consistency and adherence to the fundamentals of Louisiana heritage cuisine. The idea of Prudhomme as mentor is nothing new. Frank Brigtsen, whose eponymous restaurant is considered one of the city's best, was the first chef to work alongside Prudhomme when K-Paul's first opened for dinner. Before Emeril Lagasse became a celebrity chef, he had the good fortune to follow Prudhomme as executive chef at Commander's Palace, where the foundation of Lagasse's reputation can be found in the recipes Prudhomme developed and left behind.

While Brocato certainly learned the essentials of his craft in the Prudhomme atelier, like Brigtsen and Lagasse, he is no slavish acolyte to the K-Paul's canon. The food at Brocato's seems to feature fewer pepper blends than that at

K-Paul's, but whatever it may lack in zing is counter balanced by a depth and smokiness that serves as another level, a lower base upon which other flavors are built.

There is nothing particularly groundbreaking about the daily menus at Borcato's. They're computer print-outs on plain white copier paper and their language is simple and unadorned; adjectives are not sprinkled as freely as superfluous condiments in the menus of more affected restaurants. This straightforward honesty sets both the table and tone for whatever you order off the smallish menu.

The regular menu features seven items changed daily, and a second sheet of paper lists anywhere from six to eight daily specials. For the most part, it's Cajun plate lunch fare and it's damn good. There's fried catfish served with crawfish etouffée; Cajun rabbit jambalaya with sauce piquant; bronzed chicken; blackened redfish; shrimp and roasted corn cheese grits; a pork chop of some kind; the usual suspects in restaurants with roots in the bayous and swamps. There's always a poor boy, and on Saturday nights, they often feature barbecue specials.

Two particular dishes deserve special mention: the classic barbecue shrimp, and the crab cakes served over cheese ravioli in a crawfish cream sauce.

In New Orleans, buttery barbecue shrimp is as much a mainstay in any local chef's repertoire as Amazing Grace is to a hymnal. Created in the 1950s at Pascals' Manale and rethought by Prudhomme during his watch at Commander's Palace, it's remarkably simple: shrimp either baked (Manale) or sautéed (Prudhomme) with butter, spices and seafood stock. Brocato's take on this old standby isn't as spicy as many, but has a deeper flavor than most, suggesting that he works his sauce longer before adding the shrimp. While the gustatory variations of the Eat Dat version may not stray far from the culinary roots of the original, the result is one that easily stands side-by-side with the dish's most celebrated and often cited presentations.

When one considers the three most prominent provenances of New Orleans cuisine – Cajun, Creole and Italian – Brocato's crab cake entrée is one of the most successful integrations of all three into a single dish. The fried crab cake pays homage to the deep-frying tradition of the more rural Cajuns; the ravioli is, of course, Italian; and the buttery crawfish cream sauce could be used as an exemplar of traditional Creole technique. In all the restaurants of every ethnic background throughout a city justifiably famous for unique cuisine, very few dishes are served that so emphatically succeed in creating such an indigenous hybrid as Brocato accomplishes with his crab cakes.

In the face of Brocato's well-crafted main courses, perhaps it's splitting hairs to point out that the house salads offer room for substantial improvement. While there's nothing inherently bad about the ingredients or their preparation, the only thing that stands out about them is their complete banality. Boring iceberg lettuce and dressings that taste no different than those poured from oversized food service jars make inadequate fanfares for the dishes to come. Many years ago, I needled a restaurateur about his chintzy, unimaginative salad, only to be told he did it intentionally so people didn't fill up on salad before the entrees arrived. It's perhaps the lamest excuse I've ever heard from a restaurateur, but until Troy Brocato fixes his salads, it's one he may want to commit to memory.

When all is said and done, I like the hell out of Brocato's Eat Dat, but I readily admit to having a soft spot for out-of-the way places where the décor can most politely be called "haphazard," the ambience is decidedly downscale and the food can hold its own with any white tablecloth joint in town.

Nothing lasts forever, of course. When a kitchen is putting out food as good as Brocato's Eat Dat at about half the cost of places in the French Quarter, word will inevitably get around. At that point, Troy Brocato will have to look deep into his soul – and his bankbook – and decide how he personally chooses to define success. Here's one hungry sinner who hopes he makes a wise choice.

Brocato's Eat Dat
Louisiana Heritage Cuisine
9.2 miles from The Zero Point
8480 Morrison Road, East New Orleans
Lunch served Tuesday – Sunday, 10:30 am – 4:00 pm
Dinner served Thursday – Sunday, 5:30 PM – 9:00 pm
VISA and MasterCard accepted, no reservations
Telephone: (504) 309-3465
No website

Charlie's Seafood

When Charles and Ruth Petrossi opened the doors to
their new place on Jefferson Highway in Harahan,
the American restaurant industry as they knew it
was quite a different animal than the one into which
it would ultimately grow.

IT WAS 1951. Harry Truman was in the White House. Seven million coast-to-coast viewers made Milton Berle and Texaco Star Theater the top rated show on television. The interstate highway system hadn't made it to the drawing board yet, and it would still be another year before Harland Sanders would put a pressure cooker in the back of his car to travel the country, trying to sell his idea for quicker cooking fried chicken to skeptical café owners. Cadillac tailfins wouldn't stretch to full size for eight more years.

There was precious little different about Charlie's Seafood for its times. It was not so much a restaurant as a neighborhood café, not unlike the tens of thousands of similar establishments that sprang up during the boom years following World War II. The formula for success was straightforward: hard-working owners, good food, fair prices, family friendly. Mom and Pop were chasing, catching and carving out their slice of the American Dream.

It was a time when franchise or chain restaurants were

at best minor players in the industry. White Castle, America's first burger chain, set up shop in Wichita as a hamburger stand in 1916, sixteen years before its Southern cousin, Krystal, started selling "button burgers" in Chattanooga. A&W can trace its history back to the hot day in June 1919 when one of the company's founders sold his first mug of root beer for one nickel in Lodi, California. It wasn't until 1925 that Howard Deering Johnson would serve the first scoop of his new and richer recipe ice cream at the soda fountain of his Quincy, Massachusetts drugstore.

Consider, if you will, that when the Harahan seafood restaurant opened as "Charles Sea Foods" in 1951, mixer salesman Ray Kroc was yet to even meet the McDonald brothers, an event that wouldn't occur for another three years. It would be seven years before Pizza Hut tossed its first piece of dough, fourteen years before Subway opened the first of its current 33,000 worldwide sandwich shops, and a full eighteen years before Dave Thomas opened his first hamburger stand in Columbus, Ohio, and named it after his fourth daughter, Wendy.

Truth be told, at a time when casual family cafes were the mainstay of American dining, Charlie's Seafood was little more than another dot on the map. Harahan itself was little more than another nondescript bedroom community along a federal highway. Even the new airport in neighboring Kenner had a more colorful history (named after daredevil pilot John Moisant, who crashed quite fatally on the site in 1910 while it was still farmland).

In a decade that would come to be known for its celebration of conformity, the restaurant fit right in. Now, sixty years later, the place still leaves little to no doubt about what it is. With glass bricks flanking the corner doorway beneath a bright red sign, another faded Pepsi sign touting the oysters to be found inside and Christmas lights tracing the roofline, it's clearly a neighborhood seafood joint that has not only withstood the test of time, but also transcended it.

That's not to imply that success came instantly once the door opened or steadily as the world around it changed and the restaurant became more iconic. In the wake of Katrina, Charlie's shuttered its doors and stayed closed until a celebrated local chef got tired of having memory tug at his sleeve as he drove by twice a day.

The chef is Frank Brigtsen, whose family moved to Harahan when he was one year old and whose eponymous restaurant in Riverbend is widely regarded as one of the city's true landmarks of Louisiana Heritage cuisine. To Brigtsen, himself a James Beard Award designee, Charlie's was always his neighborhood's family eatery, if not a root source for some of his ideas about native home cooking. Passing by the vacated Charlie's as he drove back and forth to one of America's most renowned restaurants, Brigtsen found a wistful nostalgia growing in his heart for the vacated café of his childhood, where he probably ate for the first time in a different highchair. It finally got to him. He and his wife, Marna, bought the restaurant and reopened it in early July of 2009.

Two essential ingredients shared by both lionized chefs and prosperous restaurateurs are finely honed instincts and the steely determination to follow them. Brigtsen's intuition told him to change as little as possible, and he listened. In fact, the only noticeable change to the restaurant's exterior was a fresh coat of blue paint. The interior would require a little more ingenuity.

Resisting the temptation to rebuild Charlie's into a stripped down version of his flagship restaurant, Brigtsen instead made the conscious decision to keep the menu as true to its original roots as possible. There are no real surprises here. The heart of the menu is seafood, most of it cooked in a predictable manner. You'll find plates of shrimp, oysters and catfish with fries or potato salad and cole slaw with a homemade tartar sauce. There are a half dozen 12-inch poor boys and 8-inch "po'babies" to choose from, including the obligatory roast beef with gravy made from scratch.

The seafood served at Charlie's is also available grilled for the more health-conscious and boiled in season. There are the salads, gumbo, bisque and shrimp etouffée you'd expect in a mom-and-pop seafood café, and a fixed rotation of daily specials. The few surprises to be found on the menu include an oyster and artichoke au gratin, shrimp calas (Creole rice fritters), buttered pistolettes filled with dirty rice mix (but no rice itself) and handmade Cane River Meat Pies® with Creole mustard and pepper jelly.

So just what is it that lifts Charlie's Seafood above the hundreds of other similar restaurants that retain their status of "just another dot on the map?" There are two things, I think: the ironclad adamancy about both the freshness and provenance of the seafood that their purveyors cart through the door, and the enigmatic *je ne sais quoi* that separates the legendary chef from the glorified line cook.

The restaurant buys only Louisiana farm-raised or wild-caught Des Allemands catfish that is "deep-skin cut" for cleaner flavor. The shrimp is chemical-free from the Gulf Mexico. The "unwashed" oysters are harvested from meticulously inspected Louisiana beds; the blue crabs come live from Lake Ponchartrain and, on the rare occasions when live crabs are unavailable, only locally caught and processed crabmeat is used. During their short season, soft-shell crabs are delivered alive straight from the bayous. Imported seafood is quite simply not tolerated. Period.

While Brigtsen's duties at his namesake restaurant require him to spend the bulk of his time six miles from Charlie's, his influence is still felt as strongly as if he was standing in the midst of a swarm of hissing fryers and steaming pots in the kitchen. Chefs Ronald Prevost and Gabriel Beard were, of course, hand-picked by Brigtsen, as was Cane River native Janet Caldwell, who makes her Natchitoches-style meat pies by hand on site. One can only imagine the pressure they must feel to live up to the rigid standards Brigtsen used to build not so much his local restaurant as his national reputation.

It's been said that the greatest kitchens are built upon a foundation of painstaking attention to the pickiest detail, and one gets the feeling that this is precisely what is going on at Charlie's. The food is all made from scratch, which in and of itself comes as no surprise; the one piece of kitchen minutiae that spoke volumes about the place to me was that the homemade tartar sauce started out with homemade pickles.

On our first visit to Charlie's, The Sensible One opted for the "Catfish-n-Grits" from the restaurant's standing menu, a mustard and cornmeal catfish filet served with stone-ground Cheddar cheese grits and a Creole sauce. Instead of the expected plain piece of fish on a lump of grits, the presentation was more vertical than horizontal, giving the plate the overall effect of what one might more expect in a downtown white tablecloth restaurant that a resuscitated family place in suburban Harahan.

Leaning toward the shrimp etouffée until told that the day's off-menu special was a braised duck breast with gravy served over dirty rice, I was rewarded with a dish that both embodied and embraced the cooking traditions of Louisiana's early Cajun settlers. Beneath the surprisingly rich gravy, the duck could have been domesticated or shot on wing, I frankly wouldn't know which, but the flavor was wild rather than gamey and enhanced by the deep and smoky flavors of the dirty rice.

A quick glance around the unassuming dining room makes me think that Charlie's can seat roughly eighty people, give or take a few. If you're going at night, you might want to plan on an early dinner, because they don't take reservations, and as word has gotten out, the waits have become longer.

For people who, like me, grew up in the 1950s and 60s, Charlie's Seafood is a defiant refutation of the notion that there's no such thing as a time machine. It's a throwback to a time when the night skies were lit by a silvery moon instead of golden arches, an era when America liked Ike, John Wayne was big man at the box office, and it was Howdy Doody time.

Under the watchful eye of restaurateur Frank Brigtsen,

it's still possible to return to those thrilling days of yester-year, if only for an hour or two, when dinner meant sitting down with the family instead of a burger in a bag. You should plan on going before any more sand manages to trickle through the hourglass.

Charlie's Seafood
Louisiana Casual Cuisine
12.1 miles from The Zero Point
8311 Jefferson Highway in Harahan
Open Monday, 11:00 am - 2:00 pm
Tuesday-Saturday, 11:00 am - 9:00 pm
All major credit cards accepted, no reservations
Telephone: (504) 737-3700
Website: www.charliesseafoodrestaurant.com

III.
SIZE MATTERS

OH, STOP SNICKERING. It really does, and in this case, small is better. The five restaurants in this section are among the smallest in the city, resulting in food that is both prepared under the watchful eye of, and tweaked by, the chef.

While high-volume, large capacity restaurants in New Orleans (Antoine's has fourteen dining rooms, for heaven's sake) often do a commendable job of putting out consistently good food, one always has a better chance of getting a more painstakingly prepared meal from a boutique kitchen than an assembly line.

The earthy paellas coming out of the small kitchen at Lola's make early arrivals to the no-reservations restaurant mandatory. In the city that launched Popeye's, the fried chicken being served in the postage stamp of a dining room at Willie Mae's Scotch House in Treme has become a recurring staple on national television networks devoted to food. Vanessa Thurber's homemade mousse paté of liver and andouille sausage crusted in almonds and topped with a Grand Marnier sauce at Vine & Dine is an epiphany.

In a city with as large a culinary reputation as New Orleans, the hungry visitor shouldn't overlook some of its smallest gems.

Clover Grill

If you happen to be sitting at the counter
and watching the cook work,
you might even feel your arteries clog up right on the spot.

MAY YOU RELISH MY WHAT?

"May we relish your weenie?" There it was, right on the menu of the Clover Grill under the "Clover Weenie." Even though the revised menu no longer carries that, uh, proposition, the high camp iconoclasm of the Clover remains in full flower 24/7.

An openly gay greasy spoon where burgers are grilled under hubcaps, eggs are scrambled in a milkshake blender and you expect the fry-boys to break into dance at the drop of a counterman's paper cap, the Clover is the first café you'll bump into on Bourbon Street once your cross New Orleans' "Lavender Line."

Even though the signs may read St. Ann Street, the so-called Lavender Line is the unofficial border separating the bustling commercial section of the French Quarter from its quieter, more residential area with its high concentration of gay residents. Within the lower quarter is a two square-block area known as "The Fruit Loop," which is the self-described epicenter of the city's gay nightlife, attractions and events.

The Clover Grill's location on "the Loop" shares the

corner of Bourbon and Dumaine with Café Lafitte in Exile, one of the oldest gay bars in the country. One block further down Bourbon Street is Jean Lafitte's Blacksmith Shop, a picturesque pile of a tavern built circa 1772 and reputed to be the oldest continuously operated saloon in the United States. Go another block and you'll be at an all-night grocery named the QuarterMaster, but generally referred to locally as the "Nellie Deli." The bottom line is that the neighborhood is sure to make the hardest-bitten homophobe roughly as comfortable as a deacon in a cathouse.

Even though there is no question about the sexual identity of the Clover or a seeming majority of its patrons, most of the stereotypical vamping and camping is played for laughs instead of keeps. Just the same, it can be somewhat unnerving to the unsuspecting, sleepy-eyed visitor who wanders in for nothing more than breakfast when an elegantly made-up gentleman working the cash register breaks into a bumping, grinding lip-sync to The Weather Girls' rendition of *"It's Raining Men (Hallelujah)"* cascading out of the jukebox.

The Clover is a tiny place – only eleven red-topped stools at the split counter and four tables. What's more, it's visually bland. The whitewashed exterior probably hasn't changed much since 1939, the year generally thought to be when the diner opened although no one is sure enough to bet a dollar on it. There's a fading generic Coca-Cola sign at the corner and the dining room is awash in pink tile. A sign painted on the window proclaims "HAMBURGERS WORLD'S BEST." If it hadn't been plopped down in the middle of Bourbon Street, it could be anywhere else in

America.

The menu is generic – a build-your-own burger, a short order breakfast, chicken fried steak, a pork chop, waffle, omelets, some predictable sandwiches and, of course, the Clover Weenie. Scattered through the menu are about a dozen quips, the humor value of which generally falls somewhere between a groaner and out-and-out lame. "We don't eat in your bed, so please don't sleep at our table. Our chili speaks for itself...sooner or later. You can beat our prices, but you can't beat our meat." The only thing missing is a septuagenarian drummer firing off vaudeville rimshots.

It is tempting to say that the key to the Clover's success is that everything is served with a side order of attitude, but that would be inaccurate because, really, attitude is the main course. Without its sassy, brassy attitude, the Clover would be just another overlooked diner with a New Orleans address. That would be a shame, too, because the food is surprisingly good for its category.

That's not to say the food is a beautifully styled work of art when it arrives. Chances are it was slopped on a homely ceramic plate that landed at your place at the counter or table with a brusque thump. While the service is both affable and thoughtful, not to mention funny as hell at times, it isn't graceful. It will be a long time, perhaps one afternoon when there are snowball fights in Jackson Square, before any of them trade in their Clover t-shirts for tuxedos and start tossing out bon mots in French at Antoine's.

The food itself makes me think of the point in time, most likely in college, when I discovered that breakfast was more than fuel to be bolted down before dashing off to a snooze-worthy lecture. It's late night, after midnight chow, designed to soak up excess booze without making someone want another round. This is acknowledged on the Clover's website, where a mini-ad reads, "We're Open 24 Hours Because Food Tastes Better After Midnight."

The active ingredient at breakfast appears to be butter, enough butter to make a cardiologist start counting new money or TV chef Paula Deen smile. In fact, sitting on the edge of the flat-top is a tall saucepot of melted butter, into which a ladle is regularly dipped and its contents poured over eggs and grits. If you happen to be sitting at the counter and watching the cook work, you might even feel your arteries clog up right on the spot.

The scrambled eggs and omelets are remarkably light and fluffy, the result of being spun with a splash of water in an old soda parlor milkshake blender. Eggs are fried directly on the flat-top before being (surprise!) finished with butter.

There is the general assortment of meats one expects in a short order joint. Having developed a personal aversion to breakfast bacon being cooked to the point it can be snapped with my fingers, I unthinkingly told the waiter that I wanted my meat limp. Suffice it to say that the ensuing cackling and pandemonium on the part of the kitchen staff reminded me that the Clover may not have been the wisest place to make such a request.

The gimmick of hamburgers at the Clover Grill is that when they're sizzling on the flat-top, they're covered with a hubcap (always American-made, so they claim), which serves to steam the beef patty while it cooks. What results is a juicy, home-style burger with a homemade flavor, something that seems more difficult to find nowadays, when more and more restaurants cook on open grills or in broilers, and short order cafés have been replaced by fast food emporia. To loyal Clover patrons, their hubcap burger proudly serves as a defiant refutation of food writer Calvin Trillin's tenet that "anybody who doesn't think that the best hamburger place in the world is in his home town is a sissy."

In a place where waiters proudly sport ball caps emblazoned with "DIVA" and "Delta Queen," where hard-earned hangovers are nursed with strong coffee and unsuspecting tourists drop their jaws at the 24/7 floor show, the quality of the food is often overlooked. To do so at the Clover Grill would be a grave injustice. It may not be ambitious, trendy or urbane, but thank God it doesn't try to be. The Clover dishes up straight-ahead, classic American hash house chow without apology, because with solid, filling food prepared this well, apologies become needless.

Of course the place has its detractors. The Clover is totally polarizing; people may love it or loathe it, but chances are they'll never forget it. And through it all, the cooks and countermen just keep on dancing. *Hallelujah.*

The Clover Grill
Diner
0.6 miles from The Zero Point
900 Bourbon Street (at Dumaine)
Open 24/7 with no reservations
Credit cards accepted
Telephone: (504) 598-1010
Website: www.clovergrill.com

Irene's Cuisine

*It is the Old World cooking style of Europe's Mediterranean rim,
and its unpretentious execution borders on absolute perfection.*

I LIKE IRENE'S CUISINE. In fact, I like it a lot. But in one major
way, I'd like to like it a lot more.

The restaurant was originally a kitchen and two very
small dining rooms that had been partitioned out of a
parking garage at the corner of St. Philip and Chartres
Streets in the lower French Quarter. Over the years, it's
added another small dining room and a pocket bar that
serves as one purgatory – if not one hell – of a holding
area.

Some guidebooks refer to the cooking as French, while
most call it Italian, and maybe they're both right. There are
some elements of each on the short-ish menu, which should
come as no real surprise considering that traditional New
Orleans cooking, as it continually evolves, has been strongly
influenced by both early French settlers and immigrant Italians (not to mention Africans, Spaniards, Croatians,
Caribbean islanders, native Americans and, more recently,
Vietnamese among others).

While arguing about the origins of any food may be
great sport in New Orleans food circles, such arguments are

essentially unwinnable. After all, who knows for sure whether a rosemary chicken originally came out of an oven in Parma or Provence? Beyond that, who really gives a damn? Suffice it to say that if someone flatly pronounced Irene's cuisine to be among the city's best despite its apparently borderless provenance, they'd probably get very little serious argument.

It's rare enough for a restaurant's signature dish to be chicken and in the Deep South, it's even more uncommon for that chicken to be cooked any way other than fried. That said, if Irene's has a true signature dish, it would be the rosemary chicken. If not, it would certainly be in the top two or three. There's nothing very complex about the dish. In fact, it's so simple that it's become a "go to" meal for newly married couples whose culinary skills are such that a can opener presents a formidable kitchen challenge.

In the hands of Irene's kitchen staff, however, the dish is lifted from the mundane to the transcendental. Instead of using a lot of seasonings for their own sake, the kitchen sticks with the essential aromatics and balances them with precision, panache and finesse. It is the Old World cooking style of Europe's Mediterranean rim, and its unpretentious execution borders on absolute perfection.

Oddly enough, I tend to avoid pollo rosemarino and other chicken dishes beyond the confines of my own kitchen, where The Sensible One's mastery of such preparations can be auspicious, and I used to wonder why I keep ordering it at Irene's. The answer, I realized, is either a happy accident or insidious marketing, and I'm not sure which it is. You see, there is an exhaust fan on the Chartres Street side of Irene's, and starting about three o'clock in the afternoon when the kitchen is in full prep mode, the street corner becomes redolent with the smells of garlic, thyme and rosemary. It is a heady, seductive perfume to the taste buds, and it imbeds a desire for rosemary chicken that's damn near impossible to dislodge.

The bulk of the menu doesn't stray far from classic foods. You'll find escargots prepared in a traditional French manner as an appetizer, veal scaloppini finished with a reduction of Sicilian Marsala, Italian mussels marinara, even a superb San Francisco style cioppino (the American cousin to the bouillabaisse of Marseilles). All the food produced by Irene's kitchen seems to adhere to the principal of simplicity that works so well for the chicken.

One dish that gets a little more aggressive is a Louisiana soft shell crab in a crawfish cream sauce served over pasta. While not as simple or familiar to non-natives as most of the items on the menu, its preparation maintains the same confidence and restraint while adding a soupcon of traditional New Orleans to the menu.

As refined as the cooking coming out of the small kitchen may be, a major part of Irene's lure can be found in the dining rooms themselves. Each of the rooms has its own personality; one feels like a trattoria in the Tuscan countryside, another is a cozy wine cellar. The sum result is an environment exquisitely matched to the cuisine. They are small and what little space they have is as tightly packed with tables as you'll find in New York or any other major city where real estate prices border on the obscene.

While such shoulder-to-shoulder, cheek-to-jowl seating

may provoke mild claustrophobia to some diners more used to spacious dining rooms, it makes Irene's more convivial and intimate. In fact, on one of The Sensible One's and my recent visits, a woman at the next table turned and asked us if we'd ever had the Creole Cream Cheesecake for dessert, whereupon she cut off a piece and put the plate on our table with no effort at all. (Despite my mother's admonition to never take cheesecake from strangers, I'm glad we did. It was superlative.)

Service is generally good, although some of the wait staff has an unfortunate tendency to come across as imperious, but in all fairness, if I had to spend the night negotiating through such tight confines while balancing a tray of food, I have little doubt that I'd get cranky from time to time.

If I have a complaint about Irene's Cuisine, and I have a major one, it's their reservations policy, or lack of one, or the fact that if they have one at all, it's at best a moving target. According to a tourism website, Irene's policy is, "Limited reservations accepted if space is available." That's all well and good, but space is rarely available – unless you're a city resident, a known regular, and you call to tell them exactly when you're planning to show up. What little wait such friends of the house have, if any, is very short.

And if you're not a local regular?

You will be led to the small piano bar in the back of the restaurant, told there will be a short wait and you will be generally ignored. There is a small walk-up bar in a corner where the drinks aren't stiff but the prices are. The place is so small you'll feel like you're in a Nazi boxcar. To top it off, there is "entertainment" in the form of a piano player. The last time The Sensible One and I went for dinner at Irene's, we were consigned to this holding cell, where we suffered through the better part of two sets by some joker who compensated for his lack of keyboard talent with volume -- and whose voice, such as it was, almost totally disguised the songs of Dr. John, Allen Toussaint, Professor Longhair and several other New Orleans musical legends. While I am told a two-hour-plus wait is not uncommon at Irene's Cuisine, I don't know from personal experience. After an hour-and-a-half, we told the headwaiter to take our name off the list and started to leave. Wonder of wonder, miracle of miracles, our table just opened up (Gosh, imagine that).

While I understand a restaurant's need to take care of local business, the way Irene's mishandles the reservation process is not only a disgrace; it's an insult to the city's visitors. I think there are only two ways to circumvent this unfortunate system. The first is to move to New Orleans and show up often enough to become a known regular with favored nation status. The other is to show up when the door opens at 5:30. Irene's is good, but nowhere near good enough to kill two hours waiting from the chance to spend your money.

As I said earlier, I like Irene's Cuisine. The food is terrific. The rooms are charming. Several years ago, The Sensible One and I had such a lovely evening there that we went back the next night, and almost went again the night after that. Now, if they'd at least pretend to like me as much as I like them, I might consider going back. But until they clean up their act, it's a pleasure I'm disinclined to pursue.

Who knows? Maybe you'll be greeted with open arms and immediately whisked to a cozy table for one of the better meals you can get in New Orleans. It's worth a try, but plan on going early or consider taking a tent to pitch while you wait.

Consider yourself warned.

Irene's Cuisine
Trattoria / Bistro
0.7 miles from The Zero Point
539 St. Phillip Street at Charters Street
Open Monday through Saturday, 5:30 pm – 10:00 PM
All major credit cards accepted
Reservations are a fiasco, but try anyway
Telephone: (504) 528-8811
No website

Vine & Dine

Conventional wisdom suggests that
Vine & Dine has everything set up backward.

IT TOOK A FEW VISITS to Vine & Dine to realize what I found so appealing about the West Bank wine bar / deli / bistro, but once it hit me, I was whisked back to childhood wonderment.

As an adult whose middle age is rapidly receding, I remain fascinated by those Russian nesting dolls called *matroschka*, or at least the childhood variations on them. One kid version starts with a plastic egg that, once opened, reveals a smaller plastic egg that, when opened, reveals a still smaller plastic egg, a process that keeps repeating itself until the last egg is opened, revealing a plastic chicken. If I recall, there was another variation, wherein barrels replaced the eggs and a plastic monkey took the place of the chicken.

Perhaps those are quirky analogies, but should you traverse the seven consecutive components of the former pooch grooming palace, from the cheerlessly humdrum entrance to the ingeniously converted dog run secreted away at the other end, you too may find the proper words with which to describe Vine & Dine equally elusive. To wit:

1. The front entrance and foyer should be enough to

scare off anyone who doesn't know what waits inside, or at the very least consider opting for a visit to the Dry Dock Café & Bar next door. I won't mince words. The building's facade is downright ugly. From the Algiers ferry terminal about 100 yards up the hill, the generic brick building with its neon "OPEN" sign in a too-small window looks like it should house a bail bondsman instead of a bistro. There's a roofline sign identifying the business, but it looks more like an afterthought or possibly an ad for someone else. The foyer is shared with the landlord's barbershop, a place that could never be considered a "salon" or even a "style shop" by anyone other than Moe Howard of the Three Stooges. After such an inauspicious first impression...

2. ...you walk through the foyer's French doors and enter the prep room and takeout counter of the deli part of the operation. While it's certainly clean enough, and you're likely to be greeted by Vanessa, the cheerful co-owner who runs the food operation, the first time I went in, I kept thinking I had entered the wrong business through the back door.

3. Turning left, you come to a series of small, consecutive rooms, the first of which holds a refrigerated case featuring two shelves of cheeses and a small array of chilled craft and imported beers. Next to the case is a baker's rack with a modest selection of crackers and the room-temp beer that wouldn't fit in the chiller. On another wall is a table with about six types of sparkling wine for sale. It is an underwhelming start, but things begin looking up as you...

4. ...enter the next room, where you discover two longer walls of white wines, offering roughly forty to fifty varietals and blends, very few of which cost more than thirty

dollars per bottle while most cost considerably less. No one will ever confuse the inventory with that of a major wine and spirits retailer, an impression confirmed when…

5. …you reach the next room, which is devoted exclusively to reds and a small selection of ports. But it is here where Vine & Dine starts transforming itself into something more interesting than a nondescript deli and understocked wine store. In the center of the room are two small bistro tables available for customers to enjoy their wine purchases. The only time anyone sits there, however, is when the next room is crowded, because…

6. … the innermost room is a postage stamp of a wine bar that seems better suited to an off-the-main-highway village in the south of France, maybe Spain or Portugal. There's no chattering television and rarely any music of any sort. There are four tables in the softly lit, tangerine-colored room, and a microbar with five stools in the back corner. Glasses clink. Lovers whisper. A table full of longstanding friends erupts in laughter. It is an essentially unadorned room where one might be unsurprised to find a latter day Hemingway regaling a pair of unconvinced women with rollicking yarns that none of them believe. Almost unnoticed is a barred security door leading to…

7. …Vine & Dine's outdoor inner sanctum, a three-table, enclosed terrace where a skyful of stars glitters through an arbor's open crossbeams and the din of the city yields to the chirping of crickets and cicadas, interrupted only by the bellow of a passing ship's horn a scant 200 yards away on the river. Low wattage bulbs glow from beneath the rough-hewn arbor beams, but terrace's true sources of

light seem to emanate from both tabletop candles and the shimmering galaxies under heaven's vault. There are few more civilized yet casual places in the city for a glass of Cabernet, a wedge of Camembert, a nibble of prosciutto or a moonlit tryst.

Conventional wisdom suggests that Vine & Dine has everything set up backward, from its uninviting facade to its embracing jewel box of a terrace. Perhaps it does, but I can't tell you how eagerly I look forward to my earliest return. You see, despite it architectural eccentricities, Vine & Dine is ultimately a romantic hideaway retaining both the energy and charm of a work in progress. Although the place has now been open a couple of years, youthful owners Vanessa and Stephen Thurber still radiate the how-can-we-please-you attitude they doubtlessly possessed on the day they first unlocked the door. But in a legendary restaurant market as ferociously competitive as metropolitan New Orleans, making a go of it requires more than the working capital to survive lean times and the optimism that fatter times lie just ahead. It requires savvy and these two entrepreneurs seem to possess it in spades.

While their inventory of wines is short, the selections themselves are long on quality and prudently priced, demonstrating a degree of noteworthy sophistication in knowledge of both their offerings and the marketing realities of their location.

C   arry-out deli foods, including sandwiches, and retail wine sales are doubtlessly helped by its location a stone's skip from the Canal Street to Algiers ferry, but Vine & Dine's bedrock business appears to come predominantly from within walking distance. The historic district of Algiers Point may be a picturesque hotbed of architectural restoration that houses a substantial number of young professionals and their families, but at heart and checkbook, it's a middle class neighborhood.

Many of the wines are available by the glass in the wine bar and on the terrace, but full bottles may be purchased at the regular retail price with a five-dollar per bottle corkage fee instead of the traditional 210% restaurant tariff. Also, for beer aficionados, there are assorted brands from mainly boutique domestic and some better-known international breweries.

The selection of approximately two dozen cheeses was originally purchased from The St. James Cheese Company, the fashionable Uptown retailer with roots stemming directly from Paxton & Whitfield, London's oldest cheese merchant (since 1797). When Vine & Dine's success started causing inventory problems for St. James, the Thurbers set up their own supply lines. Like the wine selections, this list may appear limited in length but is shrewd in breadth.

If there is a caveat, and I can only think of one, it is that on occasion I have been in the small wine bar when several groups of ladies gathered after work and the decibel level of ear-piercing laughter kept increasing at a rate commensurate with their accelerating consumption. While such occasions are rare, they nonetheless do occur, and irascible curmudgeons like me should consider themselves duly warned.

That said, I still can think of few places I would rather be than hidden away with The Sensible One beneath the arbor beams of Vine & Dine, pencil-thin panatela in hand, watching a shooting star and waiting with a glass of tawny port as a wedge of Stilton inches its way toward room temperature. If Omar Khayyam's thousand-year-old Rubáiyát can use an updated stanza every century or two, I can think of few better places to write them. Ah, wilderness....

Vine & Dine
Wine Bar & Bistro
141 Delaronde Street, Algiers Point
Approximately 0.7 miles on foot and free ferry
from The Zero Point
Wine Bar & Bistro open Monday through Saturday,
5:00 pm – 9:00 pm
Retail Store open Monday through Friday,
3:00 pm – 9:00 pm,
Saturday, Noon – 9:00 pm
MasterCard and VISA accepted
Telephone: (504) 361-1402
Website: www.vine-dine.com

Willie Mae's Scotch House

Seven years ago, the place was an insider's secret –
a neighborhood place in a dangerous neighborhood,
dishing up plates of fried chicken with no suspicion
it was on the threshold of becoming a culinary legend
in one of America's great dining cities.

WILLIE MAE'S SCOTCH HOUSE started life as a corner tavern in 1957 in half a double shotgun house on a dicey street corner in the Fauborg Tremé section of New Orleans, the oldest African American suburb in the United States and still an area where urban re-gentrification has yet to gain a meaningful foothold.

Somewhere along the line, proprietor Willie Mae Seaton started frying chicken for the saloon's customers. And oh, chere, could Willie Mae cook.

As the decades meandered by, word slowly got around about what Willie Mae was plucking out of her cast iron skillets and deep fat fryer. Oh, sure there was a pork chop, a veal cutlet and the occasional seafood dish, but the people were coming for the chicken, with most of them choosing the place's creamy red beans and rice on the side.

Then came March 2005.

In the annual James Bead Foundation Awards, the most prestigious industry citations in the country, Willie Mae's

Scotch House was named one of America's Classics, a special designation for outstanding regional restaurants and cuisine. Traveling foodies from across the nation started including Willie Mae's on epicurean pilgrimages to the corner of St. Ann and Tonti in the Crescent City. Lines got long, then longer. The cash box filled up quicker. After 48 years, the place was an overnight success.

A short five months later came August 29. Katrina. The storm. The bitch. The collapsing levee system and water that wouldn't stop until eighty percent of one of America's signature cities was underwater. The red, spray-painted hieroglyphics on doors and walls telling of horrors lying within. The stench of forsaken death on 95-degree afternoons in a powerless city.

Willie Mae's Scotch House was not spared. Her restaurant and connected home were flooded, and Willie Mae Seaton herself was nearly ninety years old. The very notion of starting over was more than her tired bones could bear. But in a city where food grows from a topic of conversation into a hobby and finally into an obsession, the idea of life without Willie Mae's golden fried yardwalker was unbearable to the municipal belly.

What happened next bespeaks volumes about the kindness of Deep South strangers. With the spirit of an Amish country barnraising, people united only by appetites for good food and good works rolled up their sleeves, picked up often-unfamiliar tools and pitched in. Spearheaded by the Southern Foodways Alliance, a ragtag coalition of writers, chefs and everyday chowhounds dedicated to protecting the culinary traditions of the American South, an army of volunteers spent more than a year of weekends repairing and restoring the Scotch House.

Willie Mae's Scotch House reopened under the watchful eye of Willie Mae and in the more than capable hands of her great-granddaughter Kerry, the only person to whom the kitchen's secrets have ever been entrusted.

While the James Beard Award had made the restaurant famous to a small, passionate band of foodophiles, designation by Food Network as the best place for fried chicken in America, along with regular mentions from media über-chefs John Besh and Emeril Lagasse, among others, put Willie Mae's in the middle of the media mainstream.

Business is booming these days at the Scotch House. Steady streams of taxis disgorge French Quarter tourists and convention delegates at the front door, and the waits are getting longer at the no reservations, two-room restaurant. Grumblings from locals that "their" place is being overrun with outsiders are inevitable.

The Sensible One and I have made about a half dozen visits since Katrina. Has the fried chicken continue to live up to its pre-ballyhoo reputation? It has. The red beans remain as good as any I've had anywhere, and the home-squeezed lemonade makes for a remarkably refreshing washdown. The tab runs about thirty-two dollars including tax and a nice but not extravagant tip for the pleasant young gentlemen who serve us.

We have had absolutely no complaint about anything.

But these days, I'm getting scared.

While sudden success may not have killed off as many restaurants as chronic under-capitalization, it's taken out more than its fair share. Try as hard as I might to look the other way, I'm beginning to see the telltale signals of a place that has its eyes on expansion and not keeping an eye on what they already have.

Business hours are expanding. Willie Mae's is a lunch-only place with posted hours from eleven until three Monday through Saturday.

They've started to serve beer. Despite Scotch House's origins as a tavern, the place had been dry for years. While anyone who knows me might find my objection to an eatery selling beer ironic if not downright comical, there has always been a certain charm to be found in a place that makes all its money selling food. Also, a restaurateur's knowledge that he or she will succeed or fail based totally upon the quality of the food will make for a restaurateur who keeps a sharper eye on the quality of what's coming out of the kitchen.

What's more, Willie Mae's has started accepting all major credit cards. For years, the cash only status and lack of an on-premises ATM offered the amusing moment of a panicked out-of-town customer trying to choose between finding a cash machine in a dicey part of the city or facing the grim prospect of a long afternoon washing chicken grease off dishes in a crowded scullery.

I had spent great amounts of time in New Orleans over the past 35 years without ever hearing about Willie Mae's Scotch House. Now it's in nearly every tourism publication in the city with ads pushing the Food Network "Best Chicken" kudos.

Uh-oh.

It's unsporting at best to chastise restaurateurs for capitalizing on glittering reviews that start bringing in so many customers that expansion becomes inevitable. But I can think of few prospects more deplorable than Willie Mae's Scotch House opening a new location seating 200 somewhere along a soulless commercial strip in a suburb like Metairie or Kenner, the kind of place where a twenty-foot tall neon drumstick would fit right in.

I don't pretend to be smart enough to tell anyone the secret of the success Willie Mae's Scotch House is currently enjoying. My suspicion is that it's a combination of its very limited menu, dining rooms that aren't too big for its small kitchen and a dogged determination to make sure that everything is not only cooked to order, but cooked the way Willie Mae herself would were she still manning the skillets. All too often, the price of changing success is failure. A key question is whether or not the new generation, as personified by great-granddaughter Kerry Seaton, will have the patience to continue doing the same old thing in the same old way that made a small fried chicken joint in Tremé an American culinary landmark. All of us can only hope she will.

Within the time she has to make her decision, go there.

AUTHOR'S UPDATE: *Since the above was first written, I've had the chance to keep looking in on Willie Mae's with two of my "running buddies": Slider Bob and The Marlboro Man. After one of those visits, I updated my thoughts. Some of them are redundant and, for that, I ask your forbearance.*

IT WAS MORE A MATTER OF LUCK than good planning when I found my old pal "Slider" Bob on the other end of the ringing telephone, asking me the name of the fried chicken place I'm always raving about.

Slider had a delivery to make across the Mississippi River on Algiers Point, and rather than give him directions, it was easier to ask if he had an empty passenger seat. All he had to say was that he did, and that was that. It was a cloudless morning with a hint of spring in it and the lure of lunch at Willie Mae's was far more compelling than the prospect of a day wrangling nouns and verbs in advance of an ominous deadline.

To understand the appeal of such a slothful day, you should understand a little about Slider and a lot about Willie Mae's.

I can think of no better advertisement for reincarnation than the possibility of coming back for another lifetime go-round as Slider Bob. He's bald, middle-aged, undemanding and equally unassuming. He loves good food, finds it everywhere he happens to be, yet has shown the iron will to give up enough of it to lose sixty pounds without cutting a single drop from his prodigious consumption of beer.

Willie Mae Seaton opened the doors to her "Scotch House" in 1957, and proceeded to run it for the next 48 years in relative obscurity. Originally a neighborhood bar, the booze was eventually elbowed out of the way by food. Overshadowed in terms of both visibility and history by Dooky Chase's restaurant one block away, Willie Mae's remained more focused on feeding the neighborhood while Chase's built its name by feeding the New Orleans civil rights movement, for which the restaurant served as a major meeting place.

New Orleans has always been a fried chicken town (the Popeye's chain was founded here, for heaven's sake), and any discussion of whose is best can serve as the preamble to a protracted argument. Every place that fries chicken wants to put their name into the discussion, of course, but among the places most often mentioned are Dooky Chase's, Fiorella's in the French Quarter, Lil' Dizzy's on Esplanade and, of course, Willie Mae's Scotch House.

It seems that every New Orleans restaurant has both a "secret ingredient" and a determination to never reveal it, and Willie Mae's is no exception. If you buy into the legend (and why not?), you'll discover that Willie Mae passed down her closely guarded secret only to her great-granddaughter, Kerry, who runs the restaurant to this day. In a National Public Radio interview, Kerry let it slip that the secret was using a "wet batter" and salt and pepper as the only spices. This was all well and good until people started trying to duplicate the recipe at home with predictably unsuccessful results.

Had the Scotch House been located somewhere other than Tremé, there's little doubt that fame would have come quicker. New Orleans can be a very odd town, in more ways than those that are obvious. While talking about places to eat is seemingly the city's favorite sport (even more so than their beloved Saints), a lot of people have a tendency to clam up when asked about their favorite restaurant, particularly when said place isn't conventional. It's as if talking about a place will cause it to suddenly fall prey to the curse of mediocrity.

Aided by this seeming conspiracy of silence among the locals, buzz about Willie Mae's fried chicken spread at a speed that could politely be called "glacial," but spread it did, especially when Willie Mae's Scotch House won its James Beard Award. That accolade even caught the attention of Slider, who began hinting that a road trip to a chicken joint sounded like a more than acceptable adventure (provided, of course, there would be plenty of beer).

Slider and I pulled up to the non-descript, white plank building that houses Willie Mae's at about 1:30 on a weekday when business in the French Quarter was lighter than usual. Roughly a dozen diners were milling in front of the plain white door. Occasionally, the front door would open and a group of two or four diners would jostle its way through those of us clustered on the sidewalk. Invariably one of them would tell us it was worth the wait.

The doorway at Willie Mae's is interesting in and of itself since, instead of a host taking names or a formal waiting line, it runs on an ersatz honor system. Essentially, once you no longer see anyone who was there when you arrived, it's your turn. By the time Slider and I were deemed to be the next through the doorway, the cluster had once again grown to a dozen or so diners, one of whom was a middle-aged woman seemingly undone by the relative informality of the situation. When she inquired as to the whereabouts of the line, she was told she was indeed in it. Commenting that it didn't seem very organized, she was advised that (a) she was in New Orleans, and (b) for New Orleans, this was a very organized line.

Finally, Slider and I were ushered into the sanctum sanctorum, a dining room with ten tables. The room is plain. The walls are white and covered mostly with posters and photos, the most recent addition of which seems to be of President Obama. The functional, institutional furniture is more practical than pricey. The overall look is what one might expect of a neighborhood soul food place. About the only thing out of place is the framed James Beard citation inconspicuously hanging beside the front door.

The menu is simple. It's fried chicken and a half dozen sides. There are some other entrees listed, the reason why I don't know, since I've never seen anything but plates and platters of chicken make their way out the kitchen door. What's the point? This same kitchen door "research" indicated that the majority of customers picked red beans and rice as their side order. Slider fell into his "when in Rome" mindset and ordered the chicken and red beans; I've never ordered anything else at Willie Mae's and saw no reason to end a perfectly good streak.

The food at Willie Mae's is reputed to be cooked to order. Maybe it is; maybe not. Since at least ninety percent of the people coming in are ordering chicken and beans, I think it's far more likely that there are jumbo pots of beans and rice simmering on a back burner, and that chicken is being battered and dropped into hot oil as long as people are parading through the front door. Such idle speculations may be neither here nor there, since the food keeps coming out of the postage stamp of a kitchen at such a clip there isn't time or space for it to be anything but hot and fresh.

Once ordered, the wait for our food was between ten and fifteen minutes, during which time Slider Bob kept me entertained by constantly swiveling his head in expectation as a stream of plates paraded from the kitchen to other tables than ours. Our platter of chicken and plates of beans had no more hit the table when Slider grabbed a wing, trisected it and bit into the middle section.

Before the first droplet of Crystal hot sauce could land on my red beans, Slider had broken into a seraphic smile and, as I lip-synched along with him, I wondered how many thousands of people over the years had also rhapsodically claimed, "This is the best fried chicken I've every had in my life."

Is the fried chicken at Willie Mae's Scotch House indeed the "best fried chicken in America," as it has been cited on Food Network and at least suggested by the James Beard Award? I make no pretense to be an arbiter of such matters, but I can think of none better in my half century of experience, nor have I ever heard anyone walking out of Willie Mae's claim "the chicken is better at (fill-in-the-blank)." It's crisp outside, moist inside and has a taste that, while essentially unadorned, is anything but bland.

Slider and I didn't talk much as we made short work of the chicken and beans, at least until there was a single breast forlornly sitting on the platter. I split it with a knife, but much to my surprise, Slider declined to take half, sighing "If I'd known it was going to really be this good, I would have ordered a side green salad instead of the beans." With each bite I subsequently took, he somehow managed to look even more crestfallen.

Not long ago, I was reading a blog in which someone gushed that Willie Mae's should be franchised into a national chain. I'm sure the softheaded son-of-a-bitch meant it as some sort of compliment, but the factors that make Willie

Mae's such a success are anathema to such shallow enthusiasm. The place works because, by the numbers: it's ten tables small, open only 24 hours a week, defies the number one fundamental of real estate (location, location, location) and focuses 99% of its effort on preparing one item better than any other restaurant in America. And according to my old pal Slider Bob, "that puts 'em one up on any other chicken joint in the whole U.S. of A."

All I can add to that is a rousing "Amen."

Willie Mae's Scotch House
Soul Food, Fried Chicken
1.6 miles from The Zero Point
2401 St. Ann (on the corner of Tonti and St. Ann)
Lunch Monday – Saturday, 11:00 a.m. – 3:00 p.m.
Accepts major credit cards, no reservations
Telephone: (504) 822-9503
No website

Lola's

*Lola's, opened in June of 1994, has grown into
the kind of local favorite that a lot of natives
would just as soon not see in dining guides.*

WHILE SPANISH CUISINE MAY NOT BE the first kind of food you
associate with New Orleans, a quick look at the city's history will remind you that the Crescent City was a Spanish
colony in the latter third of the Eighteenth Century, the period of time when our Founding Fathers were signing the
Declaration of Independence and inventing the United
States.

Very few signs of the city's Spanish heritage remain
today, those most commonly sighted by visitors being the
panels of tile found on many French Quarter buildings identifying streets by their Spanish names.

New Orleans is, of course, one of America's true "melting
pot" cities in terms of both its people and cuisine(s). The
city's signature dish, gumbo, is a flavorful hybrid of locally
grown ingredients and the cooking traditions of France,
Spain, Africa, the West Indies and Native America, with
dashes of German, Sicilian and England tossed in to liven
the mix.

Despite Spain's influence on the city, there are surprisingly few Spanish restaurants; in fact, a recent (2009) ZAGAT

Guide listed only five. The oldest of these, Lola's, opened in June of 1994, has grown into the kind of local favorite that a lot of natives would just as soon not see in dining guides. Lola's is very small, seating approximately forty in tight quarters on a pleasant stretch of Esplanade Ridge between the New Orleans Museum of Art, the Fair Grounds thoroughbred track and Bayou St. John. Next to a neighborhood grocery market (Terranova Brothers Superette) that grinds some of the city's best Italian sausage and within easy walking distances of three other good, locally owned restaurants, Lola's is the embodiment of a place that belongs in a tree-lined residential neighborhood.

Some people think that just getting in is half the fun.

Lola's posted opening hour is 5:30 for the dinner-only bistro, but this is New Orleans, chere, where time is flexible and punctuality is optional, so don't be alarmed if the door isn't opened right on the minute.

Several guidebooks recommend arriving fifteen to twenty minutes before Lola's opens, because the place doesn't take reservations and lines form quickly. But they move quickly, too. Just the same, regulars know to bring a bottle of wine, sign up at the kiosk next to the front door and enjoy the revolving, spontaneous party on the concrete apron in front of the set-back restaurant, particularly during cooler months.

Inside, Lola's bustles. What minimal décor there is consists of brightly colored, local folk art. The tables and chairs are close together and constantly being reconfigured to accommodate the sizes of entering groups. Quarters can be so tight that at times, you'll feel as if you're sitting at the next table, at least until a member of the wait staff wedges his or her way between you with a raised tray in a newly makeshift aisle. Service personnel are casual and remarkably friendly, particularly considering how rushed they can be.

The semi-open kitchen is in the back of the house, and it's far more of a working than showcase kitchen. Mounted to the wall above the pass through are pans showing the size of paellas, the restaurant's mainstay. While the menu states that paella is available for one, two or four, the pans' sizes suggest they're referring to appetites worthy of lumberjacks coming off a hunger strike.

Despite a surprisingly long and varied menu, paella is the centerpiece of a visit to Lola's. The vibrant blend of colorful vegetables, meats and seafood cooked with rice and served family style makes this classic "peasant dish" a vivid centerpiece at the table. Available in four varieties (seafood, meat, vegetable or any combination thereof) and served in the traditional two-handled pan for which the dish is named, the paellas are redolent with layer upon layer of fresh flavors and spices.

Some self-styled connoisseurs have claimed a shortage of saffron in the dish, but considering that LaMancha saffron carries a price in excess of $300 an ounce (just a paltry $4,800 a pound or a little less than three times he price of gold), a little skimping on a dish costing around ten dollars a serving is an economic reality and a more than understandable sin. If someone wants to be a purist and really split hairs, it could be pointed out that three time-honored Spanish traditions are violated with Lola's paella: first, paella is traditionally served at midday and never after sundown; secondly, it is customarily prepared by men instead of women and, thirdly, it is traditionally eaten with fingers out of the pan itself. I have little doubt at some point during Lola's years in business, very civilized and cultured people have literally dug into their paella without benefit of manmade implements much to the horror of their neighboring and less knowledgeable diners.

In addition to paellas, Lola's substitutes pasta for short-grained rice to make fideuas, and fills out her long entrée list with garlic chicken, lamb chops with Gorgonzola, seasonal seafood dishes and more.

It has become a tradition for The Sensible One and me to split seafood paella for one after loading up on Lola's appetizers. Particular favorites include mushrooms sautéed and sizzling with garlic, and a calamari appetizer, consisting of a sautéed squid cutlet that has been matchstick sliced and served with what our waitress told us was a yellow pepper puree. The portion sizes of appetizers are generous, and their richness can make them deceptively filling, yet they are economical to the point that it can be tempting to order a passel of them and then wonder where to put the paella once it arrives at the table.

Everything is cooked to order at Lola's, which means a wait between ordering and the arrival of the appetizers. This generally short time lag is filled by the arrival of warm rolls with a garlicky whipped butter that borders on the divine. It should be noted that each extra roll beyond your initial one carries a fifty-cent price, but it's my guess that the surcharge is not levied out of chintziness on the restaurant's part, but rather to discourage unsuspecting customers from filling up before appetizers and the main event.

Along those lines, it is necessary for me to admit a lack of personal knowledge as to whether or not dessert is served at Lola's. Without a menu in front of me as I write this, the only thing for me to confess is a vague memory of a waitress asking if I wanted dessert (a flan, I believe) and my reply being the signal groan of the chronically overfed.

The menu is filled out with a selection of beers and a modest wine list, but one of the many joys of Lola's is the presence of homemade sangria, the fruity sweetness of which is delightfully refreshing as an offset to the vibrant spiciness of the cuisine itself. There is a small corkage fee for those who wish to brownbag a favorite wine of their own. Considering the amount of food and the fact that it's all cooked to order, one would think dinner at Lola's would be a protracted Bacchanalia, but the kitchen cooks fast and the wait staff hustles, so what seems like a leisurely dinner rarely lasts much longer than an hour.

It's been more than two centuries since the Spanish flag flew over New Orleans, and in that time, Iberian culinary traditions have quietly blended into the city's own. With the presence of Lola's on Esplanade, it's immensely satisfying to see those once lost traditions return to the forefront.

Lola's
Time-honored Spanish
3.9 miles from The Zero Point
3312 Esplanade Avenue
(between North Broad and North Carrolton)
Opens for dinner at 5:30 p.m. daily
No reservations are accepted
and payment is by cash only
Telephone: (504) 488-6946
No website

IV
LOWER YOUR
EXPECTATIONS

DISAPPOINTMENTS CAN BE SELF-INFLICTED, especially when a restaurant is highly recommended by someone who shares similar tastes with you, or its glittering reputation sets a bar that's impossibly high to reach.

This section is a small collection of places that failed to live up to my personal expectations for one reason or another. The causes for these failures could easily be my frame of mind at that particular time, or the restaurant simply having a bad night, or that the big build-up led to an inevitable let down.

Commander's Palace is invariably in the top two or three restaurants in customer surveys of city restaurants, yet my most recent visit to this restaurant globally renowned for its polish and elegance started with a wait behind a tour bus overflowing with a horde of visitors bedecked in shorts, T-shirts and fanny packs, and then went downhill from there.

The menu for the much vaunted breakfast at Brennan's exposed the restaurant to be little more than a clip joint with more overpriced options than Detroit can cram into a luxury automobile.

Why some people swear by (instead of at) the restaurants in this section evades me. They may be perfectly fine places where I ended up having perfectly dreadful experiences, but you may have the time of your life. I truly hope you do.

All I can say is that I got less than I expected from these restaurants, and it leads me to believe that if you'll lower your expectations of these ballyhooed establishments, you'll be far more likely to get more out of your experience.

Caveat emptor.

Brennan's

Going to Brennan's and not ordering their Bananas Foster
is like going to Radio City Music Hall and walking out
before the Rockettes go into their high kick finish.

LIKE DINNER AT ANTOINE'S, breakfast at Brennan's is the stuff of New Orleans legends – the Crescent City equivalent of lunch at New York's Four Seasons or a stone crab claw feast at Joe's in Miami.

If you collect visits to "name" restaurants, particularly those that are venerable to the point of myth, no one is going to talk you out of going to Brennan's, where you'll most likely get a perfectly adequate breakfast for an extortionate price.

As of this writing (May, 2010), the prix fixe for a three-course breakfast at Brennan's, consisting of appetizer, entrée and dessert is $36. Price, of course, is relative. While someone living in Manhattan's East Sixties may not raise an eyebrow at the idea of thirty-six bucks for breakfast, such a price will certainly raise the blood pressure of most Middle Americans, and the truth is, you'd have to examine the room service menus of a number of New Orleans' swankiest hotels to find a price anywhere near that rarefied range.

Since my main home is in a small Southern city, I'll admit to gulping once when I first saw the prix fixe, but that gulp was quickly followed by a shrug. What the hell, it's Brennan's in New Orleans, it's special, it's iconic, I haven't been here in years. Mollified by my easy rationale, I dove into the menu, and that was when the storm clouds started to brew upon my furling brow.

Brennan's is renowned for having some of the best turtle soup in America – right up there with Mandina's and K-Paul's, not to mention several other restaurants within the Brennan family's New Orleans empire. In fact, the soup is invariably my appetizer when I order it for $6.50 a cup à la carte at Dickie Brennan's Steakhouse in the French Quarter. And here it was on the Brennan's breakfast menu if I wanted to add another eight bucks to the prix fixe. What? A $6.50 à la carte cup of soup for an additional $8 on a $36 prix fixe menu? For breakfast?

Holding my soup decision in abeyance, I studied the entrée list. The vast majority of the choices were variations on Eggs Benedict, substituting such items as creamed spinach, speckled trout, salmon, a beef hash and the like. One that sounded particularly good and local was Eggs Nouvelle Orléans, where the Benedict's traditional Canadian bacon was replaced by buttery lump crabmeat. There it was, right on the menu, just before the small type advising me of the $12 additional surcharge. Suddenly, the speckled trout substitution sans surcharge seemed a lot easier to swallow.

It came as no surprise to see another surcharge; this one five bucks, for a dessert of Bananas Foster, the restaurant's signature culinary creation. In truth, Bananas Foster is a remarkably simple dish – a lengthwise sliced banana sautéed in a chafing dish with brown sugar, butter and banana liqueur.

Once cooked, a couple of shots of rum are poured into the pan, flambéed for a dash of showmanship and the entire concoction is served over and around vanilla ice cream. While the fireball's flash and audible "whoomph" no doubt garnered a lot more "oohs" and "aahs" over fifty years ago when the dish was created, it nevertheless adds a celebratory finishing touch to a breakfast that pays homage to the notion of self-indulgence. But what's five bucks in the greater scheme of things? Going to Brennan's and not ordering their Bananas Foster is like going to Radio City Music Hall and walking out before the Rockettes go into their high kick finish.

Not wanting to belabor the point about money, it is tempting at this point to start commenting on the food, which is still quite good. Unfortunately, money is the point of breakfast at Brennan's. Let's review the math.

The prix fixe breakfast is listed for $36, but an upgrade to the restaurant's renowned turtle soup is an additional eight dollars, substituting locally caught Louisiana lump crabmeat for Canadian bacon adds another twelve bucks, and the celebrated Bananas Fosters is another picture of Abe Lincoln. Add it all up and the $36 breakfast has grown by sixty-nine percent into a $61 fine print fleecing.

While The Sensible One and I were negotiating our way through the menu, a table of four was seated next to us. It took them under two minutes to look at their menus and leave. Because I live in mortal fear of being perceived as an inveterate cheapskate, all I could do was watch them with wistful envy.

The Sensible One settled on a $36 prix fixe, consisting of

Oyster Soup Brennan, Shrimp Benedict and Louisiana Chocolate Pecan Pie. Her soup was both rich and briny the way a soup with fresh oysters should be, fried shrimp replacing poached eggs in an otherwise classic Benedict provided a novel Crescent City twist on the old culinary warhorse, and her pie made up with flavor for what it may have lacked in inspiration.

For five dollars more, I ordered Creole Onion Soup, Eggs St. Charles and Bananas Foster. The only real differences I saw between traditional French onion soup and the Brennan's offering were that the Brennan's soup was slightly thicker and had a bit of a yellowish hue, which I am guessing was due more to the addition of turmeric than saffron. The egg entrée had fried trout instead of Canadian bacon under the poached eggs and Hollandaise. While there was certainly nothing wrong with the dish, it sounded more interesting than it actually turned out. The Bananas Foster were, in a word, superb, despite their final presentation being incongruously banal considering the flashy showmanship that goes into their preparation.

In addition to our breakfasts, The Sensible One and I indulged in what Brennan's refers to as "eye openers," in this case one Bloody Mary each. We passed on the website's helpful advisory that "It's traditional to have wine with breakfast at Brennan's -- we recommend: Pouilly Fuisse, Louis Jadot," since we had already found our check for $105.91 before tip to be eye opening enough.

After passing on a table in the first parlor, which has all the nondescript charm of the breakfast room at a roadside hotel, we were seated in a glassed-in room that ran alongside the restaurant's patio. It was pleasant enough, but like the fiery preparation of dessert, its wow factor seemed more suitable to times gone by. By today's standards, it was fairly ordinary.

Our young waiter, who looked like a kid going to his first prom in a rental tuxedo, was personable when he wasn't trying to be a comedian (and trying when he did). Granted, Hurricane Katrina caused the retirement, relocation or worse of many of the old, patrician waiters who had long been an integral part of the grand old New Orleans restaurants, of which Brennan's is certainly still one -- at least by reputation. Just the same, there was something both unctuous and off-putting about a young pup trying to act like he possessed the wisdom of a polished professional thirty years his senior. This was enhanced when he rather too loudly griped to a colleague about the four-dollar tip left by a businesswoman who dined simply, quickly and alone.

One of the most endearing aspects of New Orleans when compared to most American cities is its open and obvious affection for its culinary traditions. Places with long, storied histories like Antoine's (since 1840), Galatoire's (1906), Mandina's (1932) and Tujague's (1856) are not only patronized by local residents, they are revered. While Brennan's (opened in 1946) is a relative newcomer to this circle of venerability, it is also the flagship for a family of the city's better restaurants. If the restaurant expects a bright future, it needs to do more than try to live off its past.

That said, Brennan's remains a viable experience for the well-heeled traveler looking not so much for a legendary breakfast as a legendary name to drop – and one who is willing to drop more money than it's worth for the privilege.

Brennan's
Creole
0.2 miles from The Zero Point
417 Royal Street (between Conti and St. Louis Streets)
Open Monday – Friday, 9:00 a.m. – 1:00 p.m.
Saturday and Sunday, 9:00 a.m. – 2:00 p.m.
Dinner daily 6:00 p.m. – 9:00 p.m.
All major credit cards honored,
and reservations are required
Telephone: (504) 572-9711
Website: www.brennansneworleans.com

Café du Monde

*Occasionally without warning, some pour soul will sneeze
in the general direction of a plate of beignets
and trigger a blizzard.*

FEW NEW ORLEANS COMMERCIAL ESTABLISHMENTS of any
kind, let alone restaurants, are as iconic as Café du Monde.

Dating back to 1862, CdM is twenty-two years younger
than Antoine's, arguably the city's best-known, old-line
restaurant, and 128 years older than Emeril's, the first and
flagship outlet in the "BAM" Man's culinary empire.

Located at the intersection of Decatur and St. Ann
Streets on the downriver corner of historic Jackson Square,
CdM is politely called a landmark by Chamber of Commerce types and a tourist trap by those of us more outspoken than gracious. Everyone seems to go there at least once
in his or her lives, like some murky rite of passage, so you
might as well suck it up, go and get it over with.

The menu couldn't be more basic: beignets and coffee.
Yes, they have soft drinks and orange juice, too, but they
don't refer to themselves as a coffee stand for nothing.

Beignets are square pillows of dough that poof up when
tossed in the oil of a deep fryer and then finished with liberal
dustings of powdered sugar. If there is a breeze and you happen to be wearing black clothing, you may as well resign

yourself to the fact that everyone will know where you've been. Occasionally without warning, some pour soul will sneeze in the general direction of a plate of beignets and trigger a blizzard.

While iced coffee managed to sneak its way onto the menu during CdM's second century of operation, most people choose to drink it au lait (hot with scalded milk). Some more rugged types drink it as it comes or with a brimming teaspoon full of sugar, which in New Orleans parlance is often described as, "black as the devil, hot as hell and sweet as love."

My general rule of thumb is to avoid Café du Monde, which can prove problematic considering that CdM now boasts eight locations scattered across the metro area, the last seven of which most visitors bypass in favor of the original Jackson Square location (the one on which my comments are based).

While the fare is acceptable (as it should be with so short a menu), the reasons I stay away can be lumped together with the simple words, "everything else." It is a madhouse in the morning and not worth the wait, at least to me. During the afternoon and through the night when there are fewer customers, I have found the place to hover between unkempt and downright squalid. Finally, as to the waiters, while I can think of several thousand things I'd rather do than schlep beignets and café au lait to hordes of nickel counting tourists, well, I've seen cheerier folks in a proctologist's waiting room.

All that said, if you're like 99% of the visitors to New Orleans, at some point you will end up dusted with powdered sugar at Café do Monde. It's just part of the drill, somewhat akin to a Nathan's hot dog at Coney Island or a mint julep at the Kentucky Derby. Set your standards low enough and you might not be disappointed.

Café du Monde
Coffee Stand
0.6 miles from The Zero Point
800 Decatur (at St. Ann Street)
Open 24 hours daily except Christmas
No reservations and cash only
Telephone: (504) 525-4544
Website: www.cafedumonde.com

Palm Court Jazz Café

Beyond the bar and the bandstand, well,
things go straight to hell.

IMAGINE IF YOU WILL a French Quarter restaurant serving traditional New Orleans dishes accompanied by traditional New Orleans jazz played by pick-up ensembles of mainly silver haired masters.

The concept itself is unassailable, and the only thing that surprises me is that more people haven't given it a shot. After all, the Palm Court Jazz Café has managed to hang around for over twenty years running an operation that would have a life expectancy of maybe six months if it had any real competition.

Aside from the geezers on the bandstand and the occasionally heavy-handed bartender, the PCJC is the biggest disappointment I can think of in all New Orleans, or at the very least in a dead heat with The Court of Two Sisters and Mother's.

If you want to hear genuine traditional jazz played the old way and have a few drinks in the process, however, I actually do suggest the bar area at PCJC. While not as well known or picturesque as rickety Preservation Hall, the jazz is hot, the drinks are cold and chances are you won't be relegated to standing in shadows at the back of the room or jostled by the sneaker and fanny pack crowd. Moreover, the barroom/lounge is in the shorter leg of the L-shaped room and directly faces the stage, allowing patrons to see the players head-on. It truly is a good place to enjoy a set or two of America's original form of jazz.

Beyond the bar and the bandstand, well, things go straight to hell.

The longer dining room is situated in such a way that all the diners get is a stage left partial view of a few of the players, which is a poor idea for two reasons. First, by exiling food clientele to such a visual Siberia, PCJC is immediately telegraphing the notion that customer satisfaction takes a back seat to the convenience of their operation.

Secondly, and probably even more disastrous, by making it more difficult for the customer to savor the jazz, PCJC is ipso facto encouraging people to actually focus on the food, when the one ingredient that might salvage the chow is a liberal measure of distraction.

To call the food execrable may be unsporting, but accurate. Until The Sensible One and I wised up and just started watching the band from the bar, we were (mis)treated to a very respectable garlic chicken destroyed by the tepid red beans and rice accompaniment, lukewarm seafood pasta swimming is an astonishing bland "Creole sauce," and several other items that time and the mercy of a fading memory have allowed us to forget. While the somewhat lengthy menu is rife with selections from the canons of traditional Louisiana cuisine, PCJC's kitchen executions were so inconsistent and slapdash I felt I was generous when I gave their cooking a second chance, an overly charitable error in judgment I won't repeat a third time.

At its black little heart, Palm Court Jazz Café is a tourist trap that cynically uses first-rate New Orleans jazz to foist fifth-rate food on naive visitors who the house is betting won't know the difference and whose likelihood of a return visit to the city anytime soon is negligible at best. Any illusion to the contrary evaporates when the harpy in charge of the place announces it's time for everyone to "second line."

"Second lining" is a New Orleans tradition harkening back to the heydays of brass bands and jazz funerals. After marching to the cemetery to a somber dirge and entombing the dearly departed, the band breaks into joyous jazz and, with the family and main mourners in tow, form a "first line" and struts its way to a celebration of the loved one's ascension to Heaven. They are followed by the "second line," usually an unceremonious coalition of onlookers, bystanders and less than reputable acquaintances that dances along, often twirling colorful parasols or waving white handkerchiefs.

Regrettably, at Palm Court Jazz Café, the second line is patently phony and anything but spontaneous. Once the call for everyone to join in is shouted out with all the mechanical enthusiasm of a sideshow barker or a lamppost worker with sore feet, the vast majority of customers (who have no idea of what a second line might possibly be) stays firmly rooted in their bentwood chairs. I suspect that most tourists realize the PCJC version of a second line is about as authentic as a four-buck Rolex and act accordingly.

It's a shame, really.

After all, chefs can be fired and kitchens fixed. Floor plans can be rejiggered for the benefit of the customer instead of the shortsighted convenience of the house. Patrons can have their curiosity rewarded with authentic traditional jazz without having their intelligence insulted by contrived showmanship and bogus events. Ultimately, it's all a matter of treating clientele with open respect instead of cynical contempt. It's a matter of will that in the hands of Palm Court has degenerated into a matter of won't.

The corruption of such an attractive concept as good jazz and good food by such an inept group of mis-managers is more than a disappointment awaiting visitors to New Orleans. It's at best a tragedy, and it ought to be a crime.

Palm Court Jazz Cafe
Louisiana Traditional
3.3 miles from The Zero Point
1204 Decatur (at Governor Nicholls Street)
Dinner served Wednesday - Sunday, 7:00 p.m. – 11:00 p.m.
Reservations are suggested
All major credit cards honored
Telephone: (504) 525-0200
Website: www.palmcourtjazzcafe.com

Commander's Palace

Every city has a handful of very good restaurants
that used to be great ones, but now survive more on memories
of joyful events that happened there than what they offer today.

IT MUST BE ME.

For years, Commander's Palace has been regularly ranked as the most popular restaurant in New Orleans in the ZAGAT Guide surveys.

And I just don't get it.

The big, blue Victorian building has been around since 1880, when Emile Commander first opened the restaurant's doors. At that point in time, the Garden District was flourishing as home turf for the up and coming "Americans," the people of Anglo backgrounds who wanted their own corner of New Orleans, much like the Creoles had their own in the French Quarter.

The restaurant's popularity was not long in coming, and for its first forty years it gained and maintained a reputation for impeccable respectability. It was a popular location for families after church on Sundays and the genteel celebrations of the city's "carriage trade."

Shortly after the end of World War I, the upstairs areas of Commander's Palace went through quite a transformation. While downstairs with its separate entrance remained the embodiment of societal decorum, upstairs became the gathering place of choice for prospering riverboat captains and a popular rendezvous site for gentlemen and ladies with "sporting" inclinations.

When Prohibition was repealed in 1933, the need for upstairs parlors in an establishment like Commander's Palace was certainly diminished if not eradicated. Business returned to its somewhat starchy, patrician comportment and has stayed more or less the same ever since.

Commander's changed hands several times though the passing of decades until members of the highly successful Brennan family bought the restaurant in 1974 and handed it down a generation or two. Currently at the helm are first cousins Ti Adelaide Martin and Lally Brennan, who have also successfully collaborated on the combination memoir and bartender's guide *In the Land of Cocktails: Recipes and Adventures from the Cocktail Chicks.*

The Brennans made some major architectural renovations to the blue Victorian behemoth at the corners of Washington and Coliseum Streets, but the changes that reignited the restaurant's reputation for culinary leadership were the back-to-back hirings of two executive chefs, both plucked from relative obscurity but destined for global renown – Paul Prudhomme and Emeril Lagasse. It was in the kitchen at Commander's where Prudhomme was given free reign and started developing the fusion of Louisiana cuisines into a whole new category of American cooking, and Lagasse would build upon that base and develop his celebrated reputation for ingredient innovation.

While Commander's continues to maintain its reputation for culinary distinction, the true glory days have faded, although it's not entirely the establishment's own fault; after all, how many restaurants have the good fortune to hire two rising comets for the kitchen's helm once, let alone back-to-back?

It's no real feat for a place to live on its reputation, particularly in a city like New Orleans where institutional longevity is not only respected, but revered. It recalls the old joke that it takes 100 Southerners to change a light bulb; one to actually change the bulb, and 99 to stand around and talk about how great the old one was. There are any number of such old places in New Orleans that get by on memories of years past; Commander's Palace is merely one of them, along with Antoine's, The Camellia Grill, Mother's, The Court of Two Sisters and others.

These are places, particularly Antoine's and Commander's, that each should have aged gracefully into elegant grande dames, but somehow turned out to be the disheartened Miss Havisham of Dickens' Great Expectations. The real tragedy of these two noble dining institutions is that they would be considered top tier restaurants today were they not compared to their formers selves of bygone eras. Every city has a handful of very good restaurants that used to be great ones, but now survive more on memories of joyful events that happened there than what they offer today. Happy tears blur sharp vision, causing eyes to see a room through filters of gossamer nostalgia. This is equally true for customers and proprietors alike.

The restaurant even plays on this theme on its website, where it says, "That's the Commander's atmosphere; like a well run party given by old friends." I suppose that's very true if you happen to be an old friend of the house (read: longstanding regular customer), a situation made abundantly clear when The Sensible One and I had lunch there not long ago.

While it's more a matter of architecture than anything else, some of the restaurant's legendary mystique evaporated while we watched a tour bus disgorge its herd decked out in American Abroad (all the way down to the clunky jogging shoes and fanny packs). Yes, Commander's Palace is a large-scale commercial enterprise and underdressed people traveling en masse in motorcoaches have to eat, too. And yes, I'm sure I'm becoming an irascible old fart, but I find myself growing increasingly homesick for the days when gentlemen wore jackets and neckties to a major city's finer establishments (a custom I ignored once at Galatoire's and felt naked all the way through lunch).

While the herd was being seated at a long table in the downstairs dining room, which looked curiously dated and frayed around the edges despite being totally restored post-Katrina, we were led upstairs and through a labyrinth of smaller rooms into a fairly large room with glass looking into the elegantly gnarled branches of ancient trees outside.

Despite making reservations three weeks in advance, being correctly attired in jacket and tie for me, subtropical linen for The Sensible One, and being the first people led into the room, we were promptly seated at the worst table. It was in a front corner, directly next to the kitchen doors and the busboys' work area, and chattering waiters were lurking close enough behind us to induce mild attacks of claustrophobia. Yes, I realize that floor space in a successful restaurant is valuable real estate and it's inevitable that there will be a lousy table or two. It strikes me that these Siberian outposts should be held for customers thoughtless enough not to make a reservation, dress like they just got off a tour bus or are already familiar as high maintenance and low tippers.

I wondered why The Sensible One and I had been assigned such an undesirable table, until she reminded me that when making reservations my phone number was requested. The number was out-of-market, out-of-state and apparently from far enough away to avert any kind of concern about offending a local regular. Remembering the website line about "like a well run party given by old friends" made us feel like gate crashers, people who really couldn't be turned away but not really wanted, the social equivalent of one ex showing up at the other's next wedding.

It is somewhat difficult to put aside feeling like a second-class citizen, but to the restaurant's credit, everything else went more or less according to plan. It should be noted that halfway through lunch, the more than affable Lally Brennan stopped by our table while making her rounds and asked if everything was okay, but by then it was too late to request another table, so we all made nice and left it at that.

The soups (gumbo for The Sensible One, turtle for yours truly) outshone the entrées (cochon for her, fish cakes for me), no real surprise since Brennan family operations citywide are renowned for their highly regarded bisques, gumbo and soups. Dessert, which we shared, was a better than average pecan pie. We had a couple of cocktails each (including one of their notorious 25¢ lunch martinis) and our bill, including a 22% tip for our somewhat unctuous waiter, was well under a C-note, more than reasonable for a place with the reputation of Commander's Palace.

Aesthetically, Commander's Palace is in a curious place. Less than six years after Katrina and a long hiatus for renovation, the rooms are beginning to acquire a slightly shopworn look. In fact, a disproportionate part of our meal was spent trying to decide if our upstairs room overlooking the garden looked more like an old-line country club in decline (her observation) or belonged in a downtown department store right next to "Ladies' Fine Dresses" (mine).

While its food is still among the best in New Orleans, the advancements being made by the city's nouvelle garde of chefs have left Commander's cuisine in their wake, relegating it almost to a museum status (even if that museum is some kind of culinary Louvre).

Economic downturns, Katrina, the Deepwater Horizon oil spill and a general emancipation of America's fashion mores have conspired to relax standards of dress and decorum in the nation's and New Orleans' most celebrated dining establishments. Formality and starch have become casualties of our cultural changes, but with the newfound freedom of loosened collars for men and the gradual disappearance of foundations for women comes the sunset of elegance. In order to survive, our legendary restaurants are being forced to climb down from their pedestals and fight in the trenches like everyone else. Even in the best of times, it's a tough business, and these times are anything but rosy.

Elegance and tradition are without doubt two of Commander's Palace's greatest assets, but they also present the restaurant's greatest challenges. Should the Brennan family choose to once again enforce the rules and traditions that built the business, they run a real risk of losing the whole thing. If on the other hand, they completely succumb to the "casualization" of America, they endanger the cachet that has carried Commander's Palace for 130 years.

One thing is certain, however. Unless the restaurant expands the circle of people they treat like old friends, the party's over.

Commander's Palace
Traditional Creole
2.2 miles from The Zero Point
1403 Washington Avenue (at Coliseum Street)
Lunch served Monday – Friday, 11:30 a.m. - 2:00 p.m.
Dinner served Monday – Sunday, 6:30 p.m. - 10:00 p.m.
Jazz Brunch Saturday, 11:30 a.m. - 1:00 p.m.
and Sunday, 10:30 a.m. - 1:30 p.m.
Restaurant Closed Christmas Day and Mardi Gras Day
All major credit cards accepted and
reservations are strongly recommended
Business casual attire is acceptable,
jackets preferred at dinner (no shorts)
Complimentary valet service provided
Telephone: (504) 899-8221
Website: www.commanderspalace.com

The Camellia Grill

Alas, The Camellia's idyllic charm stops at the front door.

"I GUESS YOU HAD TO BE THERE."

Someone has no doubt said it to you when what they considered a side-splitting story from their past was met by your blank stare. Perhaps you and your Significant Other attended different colleges and, being the good sport you are, you allowed yourself to be dragged along on your SO's stroll down memory lane, where the landmarks meant nothing to you.

These kinds of disconnects are what I feel at The Camellia Grill on South Carrolton near St. Charles Avenue. This original location, opened in 1946 when GI's returning from World War II were opening restaurants on an almost daily basis, has in recent years been joined by outposts in Baton Rouge, Destin (Florida) and the French Quarter.

In the name of fairness, let me confess that I know nothing of the copies beyond what I've seen by looking in the windows of the French Quarter branch. My comments are based on visits to the original location, a place so mediocre I've never felt any desire, let alone need, to check out the knockoffs.

The fact that The Camellia exists in one location, let

alone four, is prima facie evidence of the tired notion that nostalgia will usually trump excellence, at least below the Mason-Dixon line. Abandoned for more than two years after being swamped by Katrina in 2005, the café's reconstruction and well camouflaged restoration was delayed by the owner's indecision about reopening, some courting of investors and the reassembly of The Camellia's displaced and far-flung staff before becoming un fait accompli. The entire process ultimately begs the question: At what point does a major effort to save a second-rate diner become first-rate folly?

Granted, The Camellia oozes curb appeal. A white-washed Greek Revival bungalow complete with classic gabled pediment and the homey touch of a white picket fence, the building is nestled beneath tall trees. The fabled St. Charles streetcar rumbles along the "neutral ground" bisecting South Carrolton in front of the restaurant. It makes for a most pleasant place to stand in line, something you will definitely be doing (and quite possibly for a long time) should you decide to visit during weekend breakfasts or brunch. Alas, The Camellia's idyllic charm stops at the front door.

Inside you'll find a serpentine lunch counter, which looks like it would be more at home in a truck stop or an old five-and-dime store, and some benches where you'll wait a little longer for stools to clear. The waiters jabber in a patois of their own, an idiosyncrasy not all that uncommon in many a city's entrenched diners and greasy spoons, but it may be of passing interest to people who have never been exposed to such nattering, at least for a minute or two.

The menu offers a predictable variety of diner specialties – burgers, chili cheese omelets, shakes, etc, -- and the food is as passable as it is uninspired. That's not to say that there's anything wrong per se with The Camellia Grill, but why anyone in a city with so many first-rate restaurants would choose such a shrine to mediocrity escapes me.

I guess I wasn't there when I needed to be, so many moons ago.

The Camellia Grill
American Diner
6.2 miles from The Zero Point
625 South Carrollton (at St. Charles Avenue)
Open seven days, 8:00 a.m. – 11:00 p.m.
Friday and Saturday hours extended to 2:00 a.m.
No reservations
All major credit cards honored
Telephone: (504) 309-2679
Website: www.camelliagrill.net

V.
WALKING DISTANCE FAVORITES

Most visitors to New Orleans will stay either in the French Quarter or across Canal Street in the Central Business or Warehouse Districts, and while that can make visiting a number of more far-flung restaurants problematic, it certainly doesn't preclude great meals reflective of the city.

To that end, here are a handful of restaurants than are in easy walking distance of the Zero Point (as are eleven others in the previous section). One, The Dry Dock, even includes a free ferry ride across the Mississippi River to Algiers Point, a little known but picturesque neighborhood dating back to 1719.

One of the relative newcomers, Restaurant August, is widely considered to be the city's top "big deal" place to dine.

Dickie Brennan's Steakhouse, just around the corner from the Zero Point, is a classic "big boy" steakhouse with just enough New Orleans flourishes to leave no doubt of its locale.

Rounding out the section are a patisserie in the quiet end of the French Quarter and one of the most famous saloons in the world – a place that was once deemed literally fit for an emperor.

The point is, while the greater New Orleans area is peppered with intriguing dining options for the adventurous visitor, in the epicenter of the city you can find local flavor around almost every corner.

Dickie Brennan's Steakhouse

*But excuse me, we're talking Dickie Brennan's Steakhouse here,
arguably the best steakhouse in a city where even prime beef
takes an undeserved back seat to seafood.*

FOR THE FIRST TWENTY YEARS I spent visiting New Orleans, I
made the mistake of avoiding steakhouses. I had been born
and raised in Omaha, the epicenter of steak country, and I
had fallen into the predictable trap of hometown chauvin-
ism. The way I see it now, that arrogance cost me twenty
years of good dining.

Most people don't associate New Orleans with steak,
which is understandable considering the city's access to fresh
seafood from Louisiana and the nearby Gulf.

It's also a shame. New Orleans is a good steak town,
perhaps not the hands down best in America, but it certainly
merits a place in the discussion.

Part of the reason for this, I think, is the old maxim that
you can almost always get a superlative steak in a restaurant
that specializes in fish, but you rarely get a great fish dinner
in a steakhouse. While the line cook at a restaurant's broiler
station may beg to differ, better chefs tend to keep a more
watchful eye on a piece of fish than they do on a steak. That
kitchen vigilance becomes a habit, the benefit of which is
visited upon other dishes, including steak, which in and of it-

self is relatively easy to prepare.

Whether or not that's true, New Orleanians have always included steak as part of their culinary heritage, and with a certain amount of success. Charlie's Steak House opened in 1932. Crescent City Steak House dates back to 1934. The international Ruth's Chris Steak House chain got its start in New Orleans in the middle 1960s, when the single mother of two mortgaged her house for $22,000 and bought the 60-seat "Chris Steak House." All retain a presence in New Orleans today, although Ruth's Chris is now headquartered in Florida and they chose not to rebuild their flagship Broad Street location after Katrina, opting instead to set up shop as a Dining Partner within the Harrah's Casino complex on Canal Street.

Like most cities, New Orleans has its share of local and chain steakhouses all over the metropolitan area, ranging from budget family places to white tablecloth, expense account outposts of the Morton's and Shula's franchise operations.

While most visitors working on limited time frames will choose to dine in restaurants featuring or famous for local seafood, from time to time nearly everyone gets a craving for the simple pleasure of a stiff drink and a thick steak. As the years have drifted by, The Sensible One and I have found ourselves satisfying these primal urges at Dickie Brennan's Steak House, particularly on Sunday nights when a lot of the city's better restaurants are dark.

Dickie's is a white tablecloth place, although its location next to the Acme Oyster Bar one-half block off the Bourbon Street strip has caused the restaurant to lower its dress standards to those you would expect in a tourism-driven district. While the website describes the dress code as Upscale Casual and claims that "coats (are) often seen, but never required," a quick look around the place will tell you that there are untold millions of people in America who never look at web pages.

Fashion atrocities aside, the French Quarter bedlam quickly recedes as you descend the stairway into a rare-for-New-Orleans basement room with a clubby atmosphere that bespeaks "big boy steak house" without ever having to raise its voice.

The service reflects the New Orleans where serving people is a profession, a career rather than a job. The bartenders pour hard into sturdy glassware, one of the telltale signs of an honest-to-God steakhouse. The dining room staff is soft-spoken and attentive albeit surprisingly young, a consequence of the well documented post-Katrina exodus by legions of the city's older, more established people in the foodservice industry.

The food is classic steakhouse fare with a New Orleans twist here and there. The headliner, of course, is beef, and it is USDA Prime whenever the meat is available in the city. With the exception of the 16-ounce prime sirloin strip, which is seared in a cast iron skillet, the steaks are grilled before being finished with a touch of Creole seasoned butter.

The operative word here is "touch," particularly in light of what has come to be known as a New Orleans style steak, the twofold disaster in which locals take great pride. At first blush steak "New Orleans style" sounds like a winner – a hot steak delivered on a sizzling platter, the sizzle caused by a pool of butter melted to within a whisker of burning. While an impressive bit of showmanship, the spattering butter can be hell on a wardrobe, and the heat of the platter keeps cooking the steak throughout dinner, rendering a steak that arrives rare on delivery into one that's medium by the last forkful. Much to their everlasting credit, the cooks at Dickie Brennan's play it straight, the USDA Prime steak maintains its specified degree of doneness and you don't walk out onto the street freckled with butter spatters.

There is, of course, the obligatory slow-roasted prime rib and a fish dish on the menu, but the knockout of the non-steaks is the Center Cut Pork Porterhouse, marinated in citrus and honey, and served with andouille and chive, all topped with a brandy apple-pecan demi-glace. It is a welcome and surprising departure from a business-as-usual steakhouse menu. There are also specials, among them a Porterhouse Veal Chop, which The Sensible One looks for when she first opens her menu.

While the entrees, salads and sides at Dickie Brennan's are fairly straightforward; the restaurant's New Orleans heritage becomes obvious in the starters and soups. The appetizer menu features a shrimp boil served with remoulade sauce, peppery New Orleans traditional barbecue shrimp, Louisiana Oysters McIlhenny (the Tabasco sauce family) and a crawfish/artichoke dip. Soups include gumbo and the turtle soup, which has become one of the calling cards of restaurants operated by the Brennan family.

As if the preceding isn't enough, there is a dessert menu. Like those at most steakhouses, the dessert menu at Dickie's is perfunctory, an afterthought for people who manage to still be hungry after a meal of epic portions. But hidden near the bottom of the dessert menu is a signature item I find impossible to resist – a seven-layer Italian cream and coconut cake in a pool of cream sauce. I never have room for it, but I always order a slice to share with The Sensible One and somehow the plate always goes back to the scullery empty. What the hell. Heaven on Seven now, pain later.

The restaurant industry is devoted, of course, to pleasure instead of pain, and throughout my life I have been advised by doctors, mentors, sages and preachers to seek moderation in all things. But excuse me, we're talking Dickie Brennan's Steakhouse here, arguably the best steakhouse in a city where even prime beef takes an undeserved back seat to seafood. So I dig in and let the doctors scream, because I can never remember whether nothing succeeds like success, or nothing exceeds like excess.

On both levels, Dickie Brennan's Steakhouse is a thundering triumph.

Dickie Brennan's Steakhouse
New Orleans Chophouse
388 feet from The Zero Point
716 Iberville Street (between Bourbon and Royal Streets)
Dinner served nightly, 5:30 p.m. -10:00 p.m.
Lunch served Friday, 11:30 a.m. - 2:30 p.m.
The Bar opens at 5:00 p.m.
All major credit cards accepted
Reservations are strongly recommended
Telephone: (504) 522.2467
Website: www.dickiebrennanssteakhouse.com

Restaurant August

Menu pretentiousness (theirs) and snickers (mine) aside,
the food was flawless in terms of both flavor and presentation,
so good that even the gushiest of adjectives would be insulting.

SOMETIMES I HEAR A FUNNY LINE and can't remember who
said or wrote it. So with apologies to the person who coined
it, when asked to define nouvelle cuisine, the joker said, "I
just paid $94 for what?"

That line popped out of my memory as I was walking
out the door after a superlative lunch at John Besh's flagship,
Restaurant August.

I'm still trying to work through my feelings about Besh
in general and August in particular. From watching Besh on
television, I think he'd be a fun guy to be around, maybe sit
on a counter with a glass of pinot noir, chatter about food
and watch him work. He seems to be an extremely affable
chap. His cookbook is terrific not only in content, but
smartly organized by season as well. I'm sure he's over it by
now, but I still think the telegenic Besh was hosed in 2007
when he came in second to Michael Symon on Food Network's *The Next Iron Chef*.

Besh is a local kid (from across Lake Pontchartrain in
Slidell) who's on the threshold of becoming a national
celebrity. It seems there's a three-step process in that busi-

ness; someone is first a chef, then a celebrity chef and ultimately a celebrity. If that were true, I'd believe Besh to be at
Step Two-and-a-Half. With a string of restaurants and his
own network cooking shows on The Learning Channel and
PBS, he may not be quite in the same room as Bobby Flay,
Emeril Lagasse, Paula Deen, Mario Batali and the like, but
he's at least rattling the doorknob.

The pure variety of his five New Orleans area restaurants is intriguing. Beyond August, he is the owner / executive
chef of Lüke, which is a step up from the traditional hotel
restaurant serving three meals a day; Besh Steak, a glitzy
chophouse in Harrah's New Orleans mega-casino; The
American Sector, which serves tricked-up comfort foods
(meatloaf, chicken-and-dumplings, hot dogs, etc,) in the National World War II Museum; and La Provence, the très romantic French country inn on the New Orleans North
Shore, where some of Besh's key formative years were spent
as an apprentice.

One of the things I like about the talented, young-ish
(he's barely into his mid-40s) Besh is his devotion to local,
Louisiana foods. In recent years, it seems every restaurant
of any note talks about its preparation of bistro-style cooking featuring locally grown ingredients; hell, linguistic variations on that theme are downright clichéd. What separates
Besh from the pack of espousers is the fact that much of the
food he cooks and serves has been grown on his properties.
He raises and butchers hogs on an acreage adjoining La
Provence; a great deal of his produce is raised on a farm he
owns near Lafayette, the heart of Louisiana's Cajun country.
In short, John Besh is one of the few restaurateurs in New

Orleans who actually walks the walk, and that's really quite admirable in my book.

But don't go getting the idea that this is a valentine to Besh.

As much as I truly admire the man, I can't help but wonder how long he will be inexorably linked to New Orleans. He already has another Lüke outpost in San Antonio and two television series will ultimately have him spending less time in his kitchens. Yes, he has chefs de cuisine overseeing all of his kitchens, and I'm guessing the former Marine is a fairly uncompromising taskmaster, but it's just not the same when you go to a headline chef restaurant only to discover that "the man" is preparing something other than your meal. It's this phenomenon that stopped the legendary Paul Prudhomme's globetrotting and brought him back closer to his kitchen, and it's what has made Lagasse more of an occasional visitor than a true hometown culinary force. That's not a knock on anybody, but an occupational hazard facing "superstar" chefs, and it would be sad for both local and visiting diners to see a talent like Besh succumb it.

Of all the restaurants in the Besh empire, August is the most European urbane. Located on the corner of Tchoupitoulas and Gravier Streets, the restaurant is a visual knockout. You'll enter a pocket bar, barely large enough to hold the few people who might be forced to wait until their reserved table is ready.

The chandeliered front room is high ceilinged and airy. There are the old exposed brick walls, which are so much a part of New Orleans architecture, and the walls on two sides are large windows that nearly reach the ceiling from roughly chair-rail height. Normally such windows are half-curtained "bistro" style, but for some reason Besh's design team chose to leave them unadorned. While The Sensible One and I weren't seated next to the windows, I think I would have found it disconcerting had we been. The fishbowl effect of passing pedestrians being able to look down at my dinner from two feet away is a sensation that strikes me as downright undesirable in a place as elegant as August.

In the center of the front room is a large stand of flowers next to what appeared to be an oversized ceramic terrine filled with champagne bottles. The tables are spaced pleasantly apart. For some reason, such an arrangement is particularly reassuring to me, saying the place is confident enough that it feels no need to wring a penny out of every square inch and to hell with the guests' comfort. Rather, it is a conducive invitation to the lazy, extended kind of lunch one might associate with Galatoire's or another of the old-line temples of Creole cuisine.

Behind the front room is an elegantly paneled jewel of a wine room, with its tables surrounded by wine racks tall enough to require stairs to a second-story catwalk. The room is darker and far more intimate than its counterpart, and could easily be considered one of the city's most romantic rooms, in that small group that would include the secluded balcony at Arnaud's, the upstairs wine pantry at Bayona, one of the postage stamp rooms at Irene's Cuisine or near the lounge's fireplace on a rainy night at Besh's La Provence.

Facing no pressing duties the rest of the day, The Sensible One and I decided to do lunch in the classic, unflappable

New Orleans style, her starting with an oaky Chardonnay, yours truly with a puckeringly crisp Boodle's martini. Our waiter, once told we intended to be leisurely, stayed out of our way, but had an almost preternatural ability to return at the very second we wanted him, the sign of impeccable service.

Over our cocktails, The Sensible One and I perused our menus, and it was at this point where the place started to lose me. I had been told that both the food and drink at August could be considered pricey, perhaps not by Parisian or Midtown Manhattan standards but certainly nudging the stratosphere for New Orleans, so I was not overly surprised when the prices on the à la carte section left me slack-jawed. To Besh's and Augusts' credit, however, everyday there is a price fixe menu offering a three-course lunch (appetizer, entrée, dessert) for the numeric designation of the year, in our case $20.11. Each course offers a choice of three selections, most of which lean toward cuisine nouvelle.

As sensible as a three course lunch for $20.11 may be, the printed menu is at once pretentious, off-putting, thoroughly affected and will send 99 out of 100 diners scurrying to their Food Lover's Companion. In case you don't believe me, look at the eight following terms used on the menu the day we were there and count the number you recognize (and tell the truth): ras el hanout, guanciale, mizuma, brandade de morue, persillade, soffrito, pana cotta, and onions (which I added at the end so everybody would score higher than zero). Such prepense, polyglot tohubuhu (Both of us can play these games, J.B.), particularly in the Deep South, can serve no other purpose than to either mean-spiritedly cow or more likely pander to the overblown egos of that second lowest form of life, the food snob.

Menu pretentiousness (theirs) and snickers (mine) aside, the food was flawless in terms of both flavor and presentation, so good that even the gushiest of adjectives would be insulting.

There was only one problem: Even though my days as an incorrigible trencherman are, alas, far behind me, I left hungry. (For the record, my three courses were, (1) pâté de campagne of La Provence pork, pickled wild mushrooms and seasonal marmalades; (2) branade de morue, ravioli nero, mint persillade and soffrito marmalade; and (3) buttermilk panna cotta, Ponchatoula strawberry comsommé and pistachios).

When the visibly small servings came to the table, I recalled many instances of being served main courses in four-inch ramekins and not being able to finish half of it due to the phenomenal richness of the food. This simply wasn't the case at August. While it may be impossible to overstate the virtues of the kitchen's wizardry, my food wasn't ultra-rich to the point it became visually deceptive. To be blunt, I found the portions to be one inch on the good side of "chintzy," although I quickly add that The Sensible One expressed no similar feelings about her lunch (pâté followed by veal grillades, finishing with custard).

With all due respect to the prodigious talents of Chef Besh and his adroit staff, I'm not certain that August rightfully belongs in a book that celebrates the more traditional and classic restaurants that most visitors associate with New Orleans. Some will no doubt argue that August is the superlative exemplar of a changing of the guard in the city's kitchens, a group that would include Gautreau's, Lilette and Stella (with a "!") among others. While I wouldn't disagree with such an assertion, nor would I hesitate to recommend it to the lovers of cuisine nouveau, I just don't think there's a historic or cultural fit between a style of cooking that's trés au courant and a tradition-bound city that for the most part is anything but.

Would I visit Restaurant August again? Yes, emphatically. But if you see me there at dinner, you can guess I'll be there as a grateful guest rather than as a prosperous host. And if you catch me there at lunch, you'd better believe I'll have a snack tucked away in my pocket.

Restaurant August
Cuisine Nouveau
0.3 miles from The Zero Point
301 Tchoupitoulas (at Gravier) Street)
Dinner served nightly, 5:00 p.m. – 10:00 p.m.
Lunch served Monday – Friday, 11:00 a.m. to 2:00 p.m.
Reservations are absolutely essential
All major credit cards honored
Telephone: (504) 299-977
Website: www.restaurantaugust.com

Arnaud's

Like all of the city's old-line restaurants,
Arnaud's reputation has been tidal,
causing the restaurant to fall in and out of favor
and fashion with the passing of decades.

SUNDAYS CAN PROVE PROBLEMATIC for visitors in cities like New Orleans, where tourism drives a significant portion of the economy, and one of the industry's major components is culinary heritage. Many of the city's better restaurants are dark. In those that remain open, chances are the head chef is cracking open a cold beer at home in front of the TV.

This caused a classic quandary: chefs need a day off while visitors still need to eat. The New Orleans solution was simple – the jazz brunch. Put together a menu of dishes simple enough that it could be produced without too much effort or risk by the line cooks and further divert the customers' attentions by having a handful of musicians play traditional Dixieland jazz as they meander table-by-table through the room(s).

No one is quite sure who should get the credit for the Sunday jazz brunch; several restaurants claim to be the originator. While any place can hire three or four jazzmen to prowl their restaurant, the true jazz brunch is generally considered the domain of New Orleans' "temples" of Creole cuisine: Antoine's, Commander's Palace, Brennan's, Brous-sard's (seasonally) and the focus of this monograph; namely, Arnaud's.

In fact, the only "grand dame" missing from the list is Galatoire's, which categorically refuses to alter its venerable menu between lunch and dinner or on any day of the week. A jazz brunch is also served (buffet style) seven days a week at The Court of Two Sisters, a naïve tourist-driven place best summed up in two words: caveat emptor.

While one can argue the fine points of which "temple" serving a traditional Sunday jazz brunch does it better or worse than the others, a closer inspection of Arnaud's, which does such a brunch as well as anybody, provides an instructive look at the inner workings of some of the city's most fabled restaurants.

Arnaud's was founded by French wine salesman Arnaud Cazenave in 1918, making it the fourth oldest of New Orleans' traditional "brand-name" restaurants. His family ran the old-line Creole eatery for sixty years before it was purchased by the Casbarian family, the fourth generation of which is currently at the helm.

Like all of the city's old-line restaurants, Arnaud's reputation has been tidal, causing the restaurant to fall in and out of favor and fashion with the passing of decades. Within two years of its founding, the fledgling restaurant was threatened by the passage of the Volstead Act, which plunged the nation into thirteen years of Prohibition. Most New Orleans restaurants surviving the "whisky drought" did so with a wink and a nod, and Arnaud's was no exception, serving bootleg hooch in coffee cups while local law enforcement officials looked the other way.

During the dry years of the 1920s, a number of the city's more fashionable restaurants (particularly Arnaud's, Commander's Palace and Galatoire's) were reputed to be quite lenient with the activities taking place in their private rooms, referred to as chambres privées. While private entrances and extremely circumspect (and very well-tipped) staff kept the activities occurring within the chambers beyond the reach of prying eyes and ears, the public rooms swirled with speculation and gossip, making eyewitness information the social currency of the day.

When Prohibition ended, and business-as-usual returned, several restaurateurs started pumping their money into immediately neighboring real estate. Buying a building at a time and connecting the rooms with labyrinthine passageways, proprietors transformed what appeared to be normal-sized restaurants judging by their exteriors into a maze of dining rooms with enormous capacity. Today, Arnaud's is a complex of a dozen different dining rooms, while Antoine's weighs in with fourteen.

And it is here where the illusions of these grand old behemoths shatter and reality sets in. To serve an enormous number of diners requires an enormous staff, an enormous kitchen, and an enormous pantry and scullery, let alone all the purveyors and logistics necessary to keep a steady stream of goods coming into the kitchen so finished meals can go out. The pure numeric volumes associated with a high-capacity food operation make meaningful customization a myth, and the heart of the high-end restaurant experience is at least the illusion of a meal individually prepared by a master chef.

Arnaud's does as good a job as any other New Orleans restaurant in disguising an assembly line approach to cooking, but isn't totally successful. This was evidenced at The Sensible One's and my most recent Sunday Jazz Brunch outing.

The Sensible One's four courses were: a half dozen oysters on the half shell, a house salad, an entrée of Savory Crabmeat Cheesecake and crème brûlée for dessert. While the oysters were fresh (and the accompanying horseradish-laden sauce met with her enthusiastic approval), her salad appeared to have come from a cloning laboratory, the crab cheesecake (good crab flavor but no crab texture) was clearly pre-cooked and sliced, and the crème brûlée in its own ramekin was plainly pulled from a cooler and finished with a quick caramelizing blast from a blowtorch.

As for mine, well, the turtle soup was watery at worst and tepid at best, the salad was off the same assembly line as The Sensible One's, and my entrée of Eggs Fauteux (poached eggs and house-smoked pompano on an English muffin with a dill-infused Hollandaise) were dead giveaways of the potential inconsistencies in mass cooking. One of the eggs was poached solid and the other's runny yolk would have run much faster if it had been served hot rather than cold. While the dessert (Strawberries Arnaud) was obviously plucked from a chiller, it was the high point of brunch; the berries were fresh and the Port sauce was tempered with cinnamon, which kept it from becoming cloying.

Despite the above two paragraphs, we have no real complaint with the food we were served at Arnaud's. The factory aspects of its preparation are understandable, if not optimal, considering the number of people the restaurant serves. Also, each of our meals was priced under thirty-two dollars for four courses, which (when compared to Antoine's or particularly Brennan's) is an extremely fair price for Sunday brunch in a classic French Quarter restaurant.

Perhaps the most enjoyable part of brunching at Arnaud's, however, is the main dining room itself. Upon entering it, one can feel the clock turning back and the tawdriness of the French Quarter's rowdiest section fade into the distance. With its white pressed tin ceiling, oak wainscoting, ceiling fans and chandeliers, the room is at once grand, but bentwood bistro furniture and Italian tile flooring offset any stiff formality. A wall of windows featuring more than 2400 panes of beveled glass allows the room to be both bright and private by day, yet twinkling and elegant after dark. Above the main dining room is a secluded mezzanine filled only with a handful of two-tops, widely reputed to be the most romantic room in the city.

Like all the "grand dame" restaurants in the city, Arnaud's has had to reluctantly change with the times. Jackets are encouraged for gentlemen, but no longer required. I believe shorts and blue jeans are discouraged, but after our recent visit, it's hard to say. Indeed, the world is a far more casual place than it was ten years ago, let alone one hundred.

That isn't to say that attention to one's wardrobe or appearance is a thoroughly lost custom. At heart, New Orleans in many ways remains an Old World enclave where many patrician natives continue to show respect to the institutions serving them by dressing for lunch or dinner in one the city's classic restaurants. And while it is perhaps a matter of age, I find myself far more comfortable blending in with those who revere the old ways of their venerated institutions than taking up with those who would downgrade them.

Arnaud's certainly has its flaws, some of them brought on by its attempt to remain a bastion of civilization in a city supported by hordes of people trying to escape it. Some flaws can be fixed – the motor-mouthed waiter trying to rush patrons through their meals, the long black skirts and ruffled collar white blouses that make the mainly African American hostesses look like plantation slaves, the picky mechanical details of making sure each table has bread and butter, and waiting to clear plates until diners are finished eating.

But the flaws are minor, the criticisms bordering on the hairsplitting. It's noon on Sunday. The bubbly is on ice. There are Sazeracs to be savored. The jazz guys are all tuned up and the army of chefs is on the march. It's time to savor the civilization. The Jazz Brunch at Arnaud's may not be perfect, but it's sure as hell one of the things that gives New Orleans its nickname of "the city that care forgot."

Arnaud's
Classic Creole
0.3 miles from The Zero Point
813 Bienville at Bourbon Street
Open for dinner Monday through Sunday from 6:00 pm
Brunch served Sunday from 11:00 am – 2:00 pm
Reservations highly recommended
All major credit card accepted
Telephone: (504) 523-5433
Website: www.arnaudsrestaurant.com

Napoleon House

*Taking a look around the main bar room
in the front of the building, one easily gets the impression
that changes have been few, if any, and that
over the past century, the total expenditure on decorations
might approach twenty bucks.*

NAPOLEON HOUSE IS MORE OF A SALOON than a restaurant, but more than that, it is perhaps the city's ultimate exemplar of democracy in action.

It's not uncommon to see local residents in business dress and tourists sporting flip-flops and fanny packs at adjacent tables blithely ignoring each other in a laissez faire environment that is more advertised than realized in "the city that care forgot."

In truth, many New Orleans residents have conceded their beloved Vieux Carré (the French Quarter) to the masses who make tourism one of the city's largest industries. Beyond an occasional foray to such bastions of the city's old ways as Galatoire's and Antoine's, or a visit to see why people are buzzing about a new chef on the block, many locals have come to regard the Quarter as a place to bring company from out of town before returning to the relative equanimity of their own neighborhoods.

With the city's carefully cultivated image as a hotbed of

decadence, drunkenness and debauchery, it should not surprise anyone when the French Quarter becomes a magnet for visitors far from home intent on giving their repressed hometown behavior a test drive or, at the very least, watch others try their hands at the wheel. In fact, it can be convincingly argued that before Las Vegas unleashed its randy "what happens in Vegas stays in Vegas" advertising campaign, New Orleans was widely regarded as America's "sin city." Considering such a pedigree, it's not difficult to see why local residents keep a wary eye on tourists; nor should it come as a surprise that their outings into the Quarter are commonly infrequent.

Yet in the heart of the packaged prurience of the French Quarter, a mere two blocks above Jackson Square on Chartres Street, is this oasis of civility, gentility and tranquility. And to many people, resident and visitor alike, there is no other place that typifies New Orleans as does the ramshackle bar that, were it in any other city, would be a likely candidate for the wrecking ball.

The 200 year-old building was originally the home of mayor Nicholas Girod, whose term in office (1812-1815) overlapped the historic Battle of New Orleans. A loyal Bonapartist, Girod offered his house as a home to Napoleon, who was in his second exile on the island of St. Helena, 1200 miles west of the African coast in the middle of the south Atlantic. Legend has it that Girod was trying to hatch a plot to spring Napoleon from captivity when "the little corporal" up and died, rendering the entire enterprise theoretical.

In 1914, the Impastato family opened their bar and restaurant in the building, where it has been in operation ever since. Taking a look around the main bar room in the front of the building, one easily gets the impression that changes have been few, if any, and that over the past century, the total expenditure on decorations might approach twenty bucks. The plaster and paint have nearly disappeared, often replaced by overlapping strata of graffiti. Paintings, posters and photographs go from fading to yellowing to thoroughly obscured by the thick brown patina arising from decades of heat, humidity and smoke.

French doors open off the St. Louis Street side of the bar room providing a view of one of the city's most notorious slave exchanges, and on pleasant days, wobbly tables and rickety chairs inch their way through them to start forming an impromptu sidewalk café, where time slows and the temptation of one more final cocktail keeps the ringside seats from turning over at a Twenty-First Century clip. Mules pull carriages filled with tourists past the St. Louis Street tables and someone listening closely to the patter of the coachmen will learn a different history of the building over the rhythmic clopping of hooves with the passing of each coach. In the midst of the city where jazz was cradled, American gospel planted its roots and a joyous Cajun zydeco beat now pounds out the front of trinket shops, Napoleon House is a defiant anachronism. The music in the bar room is big boy classical – a thundering Beethoven symphony one minute, Pavarotti powering through a Puccini aria the next – and there is a fundamental rightness to the music that is undeniable. In nearly forty years, I've never heard anyone have the temerity to suggest switching it to rock, funk or (God forbid) country. It's as if a cantankerous specter stands sentry in the room, ready to advise a musical philistine that there are several dozen other places in the Quarter that play the new stuff and the door is in the corner.

There is a smallish courtyard behind the bar room, a room to the side that once housed a bistro with a more ambitious menu than that of the saloon but has yet to reopen after Katrina, and there are also private event rooms in the 2300 square feet on the second floor that were once fit and fitted for an emperor. And while these areas are all very pleasant and New Orleans-esque in their own right, none of them bespeak the Crescent City as declaratively as the bar.

One thing missing from Napoleon House, but not really missed at all, is the ubiquitous display of photographs of people both famous and infamous who have frittered away an hour or a lazy afternoon going all the way back to the year Archduke Franz Ferdinand was shot dead in Sarajevo and the world plunged into war. While many places cover their walls with pictures of presidents and popes, silent stars of the silver screen or television's talking heads, the lack of same at Napoleon House tacitly implies that this is an egalitarian saloon, one where the owners don't give a damn who you are as long as you have enough money to buy a drink and the common sense to leave everyone else alone.

This streak of iconoclasm seems to permeate the wait staff, a polite yet slightly stand-offish crew of men in white shirts and black bow ties. Waiters whose demeanors border on the dictatorial are more of a tradition than a novelty in New Orleans to be sure, but in a venerable old joint like Napoleon House, such behavior can be oddly reassuring instead of off-putting, although it can be slightly disconcerting for men of any age, including octogenarians, to be called "young man" by a proper but excessively prissy waiter whose sexuality could easily be grounds for debate.

There is food at Napoleon House and it's far better than anyone walking through the door for the first time might expect in such a timeworn establishment. Non-cognoscenti of New Orleans' culinary traditions have no reason to know that the operators of Napoleon House are a branch of the Impastato family, which also operates a renowned epony-mous restaurant in Metairie and Sal & Judy's, a prominent Creole-Italian trattoria across Lake Pontchartrain in the Northshore village of Lacombe.

There are salads, the influences of which lean toward Italian, ten predictable poor boys and such predictable New Orleans standards as jambalaya, gumbo and red beans and rice. More unusual, at last for tavern food, are the appetizers: focaccia, bruschetta, a café charcuterie, an antipasto salad, hummus and a cheese board with six wedges of cheese, pep-peroni slices, fresh fruit and bread. Yet there is something so atmospheric and continental, not to mention appropriate, about appetizers with a European flair being served in a cen-tury old New Orleans bar with corroding pictures on the walls and Il Trovatore on the turntable.

The centerpiece of the menu, however, is the warmed Italian Muffuletta, a colossal sandwich created with ham, Genoa salami, pastrami, Swiss cheese, provolone and a gar-licky housemade olive salad piled high on the split, round loaf of thickly crusted Italian bread from which the muf-fuletta derives its name. The consensus in New Orleans is that the muffuletta was originally conceived and built in 1906 at Central Grocery Co., an Italian market founded when lower Decatur Street was the heart of the dockside Italian community and which remains in business today.

In a city where the mere expression of a personal food preference can become the flashpoint for anything from a raised voice debate to occasional fisticuffs, an argument has raged for decades about the Central Grocery muffuletta's superiority over the one served at Napoleon House and vice versa. The Central Grocery version is served at room temperature, which Napoleon House loyalists disparage as "passé," while their version is heated to the point the cheeses melt, which the Central traditionalists decry as sacrilege. It is, of course, a good-natured argument that will never be won or lost but is destined to continue as long as there is meat, cheese, olive salad, bread and two New Orleanians to squabble about it.

The specialty drink at Napoleon House is the Pimm's Cup, actually invented in England in 1840 and more traditionally associated with Wimbledon and afternoon cricket matches, a cooling blend of Pimm's No. 1 gin-based liqueur and three ounces of lemonade topped off with 7UP and garnished with cucumber. No one seems to know exactly how or when the Pimm's Cup became the saloon's liquid mascot, but in a place that takes yesteryear's events at face value, no one really needs to. Some things are just the way they are, period.

In a few short years, Napoleon House will ease into its second century as a bar. If things stay the way they are, and if the past is prologue they will, not much (if anything) will change. There might be a small print ad and an extra article or two in *The Times-Picayune*, but beyond that, the Pimm's Cups will continue to pour, the pictures will continue to age, and should a resident happen to make eye contact with a visitor there may even be a quick nod of recognition. But in a New Orleans that continues to change, who could possibly want Napoleon House to change along with it?

Raise your glass to democracy at its best. Hear, hear.

Napoleon House
Saloon
0.3 miles from The Zero Point
500 Chartres Street, (at St. Louis Street)
Monday, 11:00 a.m. - 5:30 p.m
Tuesday through Thursday, 11:00 a.m. -10:00 p.m
Friday and Saturday, 11:00 a.m. – 11:00 p.m.
All major credit cards are accepted, but no reservations
Telephone: (504) 524-9752
Website: www.napoleonhouse.com

Croissant d'Or

*...the temptation always exists to forego such conventional fare
and instead create your own buffet comprised wholly of desserts.*

IT DIDN'T TAKE MANY VISITS to New Orleans to discover my
strong preference for the "lower" French Quarter between
St. Ann and Esplanade, as opposed to the more commercial
"upper" section between Canal Street and Jackson Square.
With the exception of Decatur Street and the bustling
French Market, the lower Quarter is quieter, more residential and generally easier on all the senses.

It's far cleaner than the five main blocks of the Bourbon Street zoo. It certainly smells fresher, and chances are
your foot won't stick in something tossed onto the sidewalk.
You can actually hear the clopping hooves of the mules
pulling the open-air tourist carriages, and if you listen carefully, you can eavesdrop on the drivers as they mangle the
true history of New Orleans in favor of yarns, gossip and
outright whoppers.

For years, I've read and heard about New Orleans being
"the most European city in America" (however you may
wish to interpret such an open-ended clause), and having
traveled a great part of the European continent, I'm inclined
to agree. The Euro-vibe notion is particularly true in the
lower Quarter, and it's one of the main reasons The Sensi-

ble One and I decided to make our first "second home" on Esplanade before Katrina.

The area features an abundance of boutique hotels (among them Le Richelieu, Soniat House, the Provincial and others) and cozy restaurants (Irene's Cuisine, Stella!, Italian Barrel and more), but the place I find myself repeatedly coming back to is Croissant D'or, a pocket patisserie on a quiet stretch of Ursulines Avenue between Chartres and Royal Streets.

At first glance, Croissant D'or is little more than a storefront coffee shop catering to the neighborhood's early risers and shopkeepers. While it looks pleasant enough from the sidewalk, it's the kind of place people have a tendency to pass by. It's rarely full. In fact, I've been going there for over a quarter century and can't recall ever having to wait for a table.

The inside is attractive in a Euro-retro kind of way. In a previous life, it was the original home of Angelo Brocato's Italian ice cream parlor and bakery; at least until the city's leading gelato maker joined the migration of the city's Italian population from the lower Quarter into the Mid-City neighborhood. The tile remains Italianate in inspiration, the lights inside the main archway's rim are evocative of an early 20th Century ice cream emporium, and the white tablecloths contrasting against the dark, utilitarian furniture gives Croissant D'or a classic French bistro casual feeling.

The main room, bisected by the arch, has the counter and bakery cases at one end and, at the other, a large stained-glass wall panel identifying itself as "The Coffee House," which I gather was either the name of a previous incarnation or perhaps a piece salvaged from a different restaurant that went belly up years ago. It's a small room, perhaps a dozen tables, but outside several more tables are available on a petite open-air patio with a burbling fountain. Despite intermittent visits by the occasional pigeon in search of a runaway crumb or two, the place oozes charm.

Tucked away out of sight behind the main counter is the very heart of Croissant D'or, its bakery, and its output borders on the divine. The namesake croissants are flaky, delicate and as golden as the patisserie's name suggests. Rather than list an exhaustive inventory, suffice it to say that if it can be done with, on or to a croissant, you'll find it there. Savory with sausage, sweet with almond or stuffed with chicken salad and served as a sandwich, the croissants are versatile, but merely the beginning. There is usually a selection of quiches, a kettle or two of soup and sandwiches prepared on small baguettes baked on premises in the traditional French manner.

As well prepared as all the mainstream lunch items may be, the temptation always exists to forego such conventional fare and instead create your own buffet comprised wholly of desserts. A number of years ago, it was said that a major part of Croissant D'or sales came from providing desserts to numerous restaurants around the city. Whether or not that remains true today, I am in no position to say; nonetheless, their inventory doesn't seem to be as large or extensive as I remember from the pre-Katrina days. I can say without hesitation, however, that Croissant D'or serves some of New Orleans' most beautifully constructed and presented French pastries.

One of the front baker's cases is filled with nothing but desserts. Napoleons, casinos, fruit-laden tarts, éclairs, carrot cake and numerous other delectables fight for your attention in an array that can prove to be mesmerizing. When the line at the counter is long enough, I can normally decide on a single choice. This has taught me to wish for short lines, which allow me to select several desserts and justify it by declaring that customers behind me shouldn't be forced to wait on account of my indecision.

Oddly enough, in the face of all the mainstream items and decadent patisserie offerings, my favorite thing at Croissant D'or is a simple peasant's breakfast: a cup of black coffee, a modest baguette and enough soft butter to literally slather it. In direct contrast to what the pastries demonstrate in terms of culinary showmanship, there is a straightforward simplicity in the baguette that creates an elegance all its own. Holistically, it provides a most agreeable way to begin a day in a city that portends undiscovered gastronomic treasures running deep into the night.

Within the tight confines of Croissant D'or, there isn't a lot of people watching. Most people seem content to keep their nose in the morning newspaper and their index finger curled around the handle of their white ceramic coffee cup. For a room with floor-to-ceiling tile walls, it is conspicuously quiet; the anticipated echo is smothered by soft conversation. The end result is unexpectedly disarming.

In the end, there is a fundamental rightness to Croissant D'or. Even though this French patisserie makes its home in a reclaimed Italian ice cream parlor, one gets the sense that the city grew around it, that the gentle European flavor of the lower Quarter is an outgrowth of the place instead of its host.

It was in this room and on the hidden patio where The Sensible One and I began to feel at one with the people in the quieter, gentler neighborhoods in this remarkable city of villages. Now, years later, we not only feel at one, we feel at home.

Croissant D'or
French Patisserie
0.7 miles from The Zero Point
617 Ursulines Avenue
Open Wednesday through Monday, 6:30 am – 3:00 pm
No reservations; Accepts all major credit cards
Telephone: (504) 524-4663
No website

The Dry Dock Café & Bar

*The Dry Dock is a friendly, comfortable bar
that serves food with a local flavor, and there are times
when no one wants anything more than just that.*

AT THE FOOT OF CANAL STREET, next to the Aquarium of the
Americas, you'll find the entrance to the Canal Street Ferry,
one of my favorite places to kill a spring or autumn afternoon.

It's not much of a ride, taking about ten minutes to
chug across the Mississippi River to the West Bank, and the
terminal, particularly on the New Orleans side, is a depress-
ing specimen of municipal architecture. An industrial, institutional pile, the first thing the terminal makes me think
about is how out of place it looks in a city devoted to pleas-
ures of the senses.

Once you board the ferry on its upper deck, negotiate
your way down the steep stairway to the auto deck and
make your way to the uncovered end of the boat. It seems
that even on days when the heat covers the city like a wet
wool blanket, there's still a breeze on the mighty Mississippi,
and as the wind tousles your hair, you have the opportunity
to lean against a rail and behold one of the better views of
the city. The historic French Market and the triple spires of
St. Louis Cathedral define the Vieux Carré and to their left

rise the towers of downtown. A bevy of ships pass by, from barges to tankers to cruise ships, and even the sternwheeler Natchez glides past like a wedding cake on the waters with her rolling paddles and piping calliope. It is truly a way to start feeling at one with the 300-year history of New Orleans and the river that has forever been her lifeblood.

Better still, it doesn't cost a nickel.

Once you disembark, you'll be in Algiers Point, a town that was born in New Orleans' infancy. Over time, Algiers Point has been a railhead, home to shipyards, naval stations and even the Civil War powder magazine for her sister city. Until the "Crescent City Connection" bridge was completed in 1958, the Point was most accessible by the ferry and remained a small and sleepy town. That small town character remains today, when one can walk the levee around the tightest bend in the Mississippi River, look one way and see a shimmering cityscape, then look the other direction into a neighborhood dotted with Victorian era housing and an unforeseen number of steeples.

Down the hill from the ferry terminal is the Dry Dock Café & Bar, a blue gray frame building with striped awnings on the windows and three outdoor tables under thatched patio umbrellas. It's an unassuming place both outside and in.

There's a small bar in front and a medium sized restaurant behind it. A quick glance at the bar leads one to believe that the house drink is most likely bottled beer. The restaurant side of the room is green and covered with décor that appears to have straggled in one item at a time compliments of regular customers, and then filled in by friendly breweries. In the corner is a tall spiral stairwell going who knows where.

The Dry Dock's menu is longer than one might expect, but it isn't all that ambitious. It's mainly pub grub, Louisiana style – poor boys, gumbo, salads, about a dozen lunch plates and a list of bar munchies designed to keep the deep fat fryer busy. Were it not for the food's New Orleans accent, the Dry Dock could be a nondescript bar in most small coastal towns on any American coast.

Truth be told, I don't give a damn. The Dry Dock is a friendly, comfortable bar that serves food with a local flavor, and there are times when no one wants anything more than just that. The old Chinese proverb is, "The journey is the reward," and the Dry Dock makes a genial halfway house on one of the city's most pleasant outings.

The Dry Dock Café & Bar
Neighborhood Tavern
0.7 miles from The Zero Point
133 Delaronde Street
(One block from the Algiers Point Ferry)
Restaurant Hours: 11:00 a.m. – 10:00 p.m;
Sunday, 11:00 a.m. – 9:00 p.m.
Bar Hours: 11:00 a.m. - until…
Major credit cards accepted
Telephone: (504) 361-8240
Website: www.thedrydockcafe.com

APPENDIX

You Haven't Heard the Last of Me....

On the cover of this guidebook, you no doubt saw it was the "2012 Edition." The reason for this is so you won't confuse it with the 2013 edition, which is planned for a release during the holiday season before.

I bring this up not only as a blatant plug for the next edition but in hopes that you'll help me make it even more helpful than this one.

Several times throughout this book it's been stated that arguing about New Orleans restaurants is one of the city's major sports. I'd be honored if you'd join the fight.

Should you take any of the recommendations in this book and think I'm crazy, I want you to tell me.

Should you know of a place that the rest of the world needs to learn about, drop me line.

Should you be a restaurateur plugging your own place, that's okay, too. We all have to sell our wares; all I ask is that not only do you proudly sing your own praises, tell me where you like to go to lunch or dinner on your rare days off.

There are two easy ways to reach me:

First, my e-mail is: mail@stevenwellshicks.com

Second, my blog is: hickwrites.blogspot.com

Depending upon the volume of e-mail, I'll try to respond in person (but no promises). I do promise, however, to keep your thoughts in mind as the 2013 edition gets ready to go to press.

In advance, thanks.

A Most Informal Bibliography

The main source for the material in this book is my memory, a commodity that is subject to any number of flaws: misreading of a situation as it occurs, misinterpretation after the fact, unconscious revision with the passage of time, filtration through personal bias, and other factors no doubt too numerous to list.

Of course, the Internet was useful, too. Restaurant websites (listed at the bottom of each individual profile) were used for basic factual information, such as addresses and operations, verification of menu offerings, dates and history.

Two websites I found particularly helpful were: www.nolamenu.com, which is e-published several times a week by New Orleans restaurant critic Tom Fitzmorris, and www.nola.com/dining-guide/, the web extension of *The Times Picayune*, New Orleans' major daily. While the main audience for both these sites is predominantly local rather than geared toward the short-term visitor, they are both valuable resources for factual information. Like mine, the opinions they present are strictly their own, so take them for what they're worth.

Along the way, I found myself chasing down factoids and technical cooking information at any number of sites, among them those produced by The Food Network, The New York Times and several dozen sites I found by stubbornly linking from one to the next.

Helpful books about the city and its restaurants include (but are not limited to):

Rohen, Sara, *Gumbo Tales, Finding My Place at the New Orleans Table*, W.W. Norton & Company, 2008

Compilation, *Hungry? Thirsty? New Orleans: The Lowdown on Where the Real People Eat and Drink*, Hungry City Guides, 2009

Compilation, *ZAGAT New Orleans 2009*, ZAGAT Surveys, 2008

Johnson, Pableaux, *Eating New Orleans: From French Quarter Creole Dining to the Perfect Poboy*, The Countryman Press, 2005

Books consulted regarding identified chefs or Louisiana cooking techniques include:

Prudhomme, Paul, *Chef Paul Prudhomme's Louisiana Kitchen*, William Morrow Cookbooks, 1984

Spicer, Susan with Paula Drisbrowe, *Crescent City Cooking: Unforgettable Recipes from Susan Spicer's New Orleans*, Knopf, 2007

Link, Donald with Paula Drisbrowe, *Real Cajun: Rustic Home Cooking from Donald Link's Louisiana*, Clarkson Potter, 2009

Besh, John, *My New Orleans: The Cookbook*, Andrews McMeel

Publishing, 2009

Rodrigue, Melvin with Jyl Benson, *Galatoire's Cookbook: Recipes and Family History from the Time-Honored New Orleans Restaurant*, Clarkson Potter, 2005

Galatoire, Leon, *Leon Galatoire's Cookbook*, Pelican Publishing, 1994

Brennan, Ralph and Gene Bourg, *Ralph Brennan's New Orleans Seafood Cookbook*, Vissi D'Arte Books, 2008

Folse, John D., *The Encyclopedia of Cajun & Creole Cuisine*, Chef John Folse & Company Publishing, 2004

In assembling the manuscript, all efforts were made to avoid the direct quotation of passages from the above-mentioned or other references. Any similarities were unintentional and/or unavoidable. I apologize for anything another author or his/her publisher feels may be otherwise, and I further apologize to any authors or publishers who feel they were not credited for contributions; such an exclusion was by no means intentional. Where information is anecdotal or apocryphal, it has been so labeled within the guidebook. In cases where references differ and were irreconcilable on factual matter, I did my best to select the version that seemed to make the most sense.

Acknowledgements

Special thanks to The Sensible One, Lil McKinnon Hicks, dinner companion, champagne buddy, indefatigable sounding board, editor and conscience.

Every author needs a cheering section and mine has included: Mike Ellis, Marshall Magee, Hal McCarley, Eric Ray, Jackie Ray, Rosemary Hall, Tom Dupree, Cecily Stevens, Bill Andrews, Laurie Taylor, Kim Brooks, Elizabeth Browne and "Slider Bob" Wilson.

This book would run several thousand pages if I tried to include all the chefs, bartenders, servers, busboys, scullery slaves and hosts who have made the many times I have spent at New Orleans tables the times of my life. Though I will never know your names and you will never know my face, my heartfelt thanks for all you've done in the past and will in the future. If only I could cajole Gail and Anthony Uglesich out of retirement, and figure out how to bring the late Louis LaFleur back across the River Styx, life would be perfect.

About the Author

Steven Wells Hicks is a recovering advertising and marketing research executive who divides his time between homes in the Mississippi heartland and New Orleans' historic Algiers Point neighborhood. He is the author of three novels: The Gleaner, a love story; The Fall of Adam, a satire of advertising and the state of Mississippi; and Horizontal Adjustment, a politically incorrect comedy about TV news, crooked televangelists, sex and the Redneck Riviera.

CPSIA information can be obtained at www.ICGtesting.com
Printed in the USA
BVOW021414190312

285534BV00009B/35/P

9 781468 065671